Inspired

The Stories of Nine Solo Female Travelers

Chelsey Schultz

Collaborator

~~~

Authors
Jennifer Armstrong
Katie Birtles
Daisy Busker
Sarah Haringcaspel
Akanksha Holani
Sarah Kilbourne
Kaitlyn Knoll
Daniela Ramos
Chelsey Schultz

Copyright © 2018 Chelsey Schultz

All rights reserved.

This book or any portion thereof may not be reproduced or used in any manner whatsoever without the express written permission of the authors except for the use of brief quotations in a book review.

www.theninjagypsy.com

Editors
Jordan Thompson
Kim Olsen

Cover Artist
Esther Alice Romanoff

First Edition

ISBN 9781733530606

Praise for *Inspired*

"These brave women will want to make you see the world and if you can't they bring their experiences to you. I laughed and cried with them. This is an amazing book for those who love and live to travel."
- Kary

"What a terrific read – one that should be read by all intrepid travelers, inasmuch as it's directed towards the solo female traveler, there are many helpful guidelines all should follow when following the path of self-determination.
The book of nine diverse female travelers, reflecting on their experiences, each detailing their joy (and a few complications) of seeing, doing and going to incredible places in this amazing world – living life at its fullest – which most will never have the chance to do. They have each dared to travel solo to far-flung destinations, fortunate enough to meet kindred spirits along the way. Learning that only way to really see what is there is to talk with others who are on the same path." - Dan

"LOVED THIS BOOK!! Perfect for anyone hesitant about traveling. The stories of these 9 ladies will definitely 'Inspire' you to get out and explore the world we live in. A must read this summer."
- Leslie

"Inspired: The Story of Nine Solo Female Travelers by Chelsey Schultz was an interesting read. Each traveler told their story of traveling to different countries alone and shared their experiences. It was seen through their own eyes and each one was different. I happened to like the last story the best. It was well written and the author made you feel you were traveling with her and experienced the travels as she did." – Marina

"A wonderful book filled with interesting snippets of women experiencing the world on solo journeys. Great stories. Amazing women. With a clear message that you can do it, too!" - Clyde

"Please get this book if you are in your early twenties (or have a daughter in her early twenties). It is like 9 travel novels all in one! I didn't realize until I started reading it how much of a 'scary unknown' traveling was for me and how much I was holding myself back by not doing it. I desperately wanted to and yet it didn't seem feasible. I want to say a HUGE thank you for every writer that had a part of making this book (and the wonderful pictures, too). Reading the first-hand accounts from women who have traveled long distances made an impact on me. They weren't shy to say that there are obstacles to cross and things to be aware of when traveling, but they also made it clear that it was possible and extremely rewarding if you take the leap. If these 9 women can do it, then I can do it too."
- Esther

"I read this book just after having a few detailed conversations with female friends about the differences in traveling as a male or female. I knew there were differences but I couldn't truly gain a perspective until reading this book and these stories from these free-spirited women.
Funny, scary and adventurous, these women have some excellent stories to tell from guest house nightmares to hitchhiking adventures to African tribal experiences; it seems they cover every bit of the world in these excellent pieces.
As a long-time dude solo traveler, I can 100% recommend this to any guy looking for a better glimpse at why solo traveling as a woman is something even more courageous and special than what we are doing. Excellent work!" - Adam

> Bailey,
> The world is full of adventures waiting for you to discover. Take advantage of this precious time of your life to go after them. Be bold, be brave, be wise.
> Love,
> Chelsey S.

To all the women you have ever wanted to travel.

"We travel not to escape life, but for life not to escape us." ~
Anonymous

CONTENTS

My Journey Through Asia (And To Myself)
    by Kaitlyn Knoll 1
No Hurry to Get Home
    by Daniela Ramos 21
Silent Witness
    by Jennifer Armstrong...........................43
To All the Warriors I May One Day Meet
    by Sarah Haringcaspel 65
The Truths and Dares of Travel
    by Akanksha Holani...............................93
From Suburbs to Sightseeing: One Woman's Road to Solo Travel
    by Sarah Kilbourne 113
The Travelling Sarcastic Goes Solo
    by Daisy Busker....................................139
I Was Here
    by Katie Birtles 175
Thinking Outside the Box
    by Chelsey Schultz...............................203

My Journey Through Asia (And To Myself)

by Kaitlyn Knoll

My journey of solo travel started at the young age of nineteen. Previously, I had always loved the idea of traveling alone-the freedom, the adventure, and most of all-the exhilaration of arriving somewhere new. I was enthralled by the concept of throwing off the safety net of comfort and forging into the unknown. In junior high, I would pore over dog-eared copies of the travel bible, otherwise known as Lonely Planet. While other girls were visualizing their dream weddings, I was imagining myself wandering back streets in foreign marketplaces, hiking through exotic jungles, and having adventures that I knew were out there waiting for me.

Alas, I knew I would have to wait.

Throughout high school, I worked as a barista to save up money for travel. Waking up
at 4am to make lattes was painful, but I knew that the goal on the other side of the fence (or the world) was worth it. I grew up in a smaller town, and most of my friends and family thought a young girl backpacking Asia by herself was pretty foolish and stupid. However, I was convinced that I was going to Asia-and I was going

to go alone. I bought my ticket to Bangkok, packed up a small backpack, and decided I wasn't going to plan anything-not even the guesthouse on my first night.

My bravery ended at the airport. I convinced myself I lost my debit card (it was in my wallet the whole time) and called my mom in tears. *My poor mother.*

However, I boarded the plane, and proceeded to have my very first solo backpacking trip. When I arrived in Bangkok, I headed immediately for the backpackers' ghetto that is Khao San Road. Vendors selling embalmed scorpions, tuk-tuk drivers beeping, and the smells of spices and incense overwhelmed my senses. For more experienced backpackers, this place is seen as a mandatory pit stop where you can stock up on western amenities before heading off to more adventurous destinations. For me, it was exotic and overwhelming. I wandered down the street looking like a lost puppy until your typical dreadlocked hippie came over to me and pointed at a hostel, citing that it was "cheap and 'not so clean', but cheap!" And so, the adventure began.

Before the age of smart phones, I had to go to internet cafes to let my friends and family know I was safe. I didn't book hotels on TripAdvisor-I just showed up, bedraggled from 10-hour bus rides, and hoped for the best. Those four months in Southeast Asia taught me more than I can wrap my head around. I made friendships I will never forget, learned about my own strength, and realized that most people are pretty good at heart.

Hiking always grounds me and gives me the courage and strength to face my fears.

That trip planted a seed in me that grew and took root. When I graduated college at 22, I moved to Thailand and have been abroad since. I've had adventures, epic loves, and learned lessons from the road that will stick with me for the rest of my life. My experiences on the road have all been valuable. However, it's been far from easy. A few lessons were humbling, and most came at unlikely times and from unlikely people. There have been times when I regretted my decision to travel the world, and times when I was filled with gratitude so immense that my heart could burst. That being said, I wouldn't change my experiences for the world.

Fearlessness

I had my first brush with real fear backpacking on my first solo trip.

I had just arrived in the small Cambodian town, Kampot. I was already feeling flustered, as our bus had broken down on the drive and I had spent the past 8 hours sweating on the side of the road waiting for the driver to fix the engine. When we arrived in Kampot, it was pretty late. I was so ready to have a shower and a relaxing night in.

However, the universe had other plans for me.

I asked a motorcycle driver to take me to Bodhi Villa, which was supposed to be a backpacker's paradise. He claimed to not know where it was and took me took his friend's guesthouse instead. I knew this was a scam, but I was so tired at that point I didn't care. When we arrived at his friend's (extremely rural) hostel, I was greeted by a short, skinny little Cambodian man who showed me to my room.

He was giving off slightly creepy vibes, but I ignored it and told him goodnight. About 10 minutes later, I heard a light tapping on my door. I wanted to claim ignorance and pretend I wasn't there, but to my knowledge, I was the only other guest and I was obviously in the room.

I opened the door and saw him standing there with two beer bottles. He asked me if I would have a quick drink with him, and I didn't want be rude, so I said yes.

Our conversation started out innocently enough, but then he started asking me if I had a boyfriend. I told him that I did (I didn't), and then he asked my birthday. When I told him, he looked at me with this weird little grin and said, *"That's my dead girlfriend's birthday."*

When I asked him what happened, he responded, *"Accident."*

I tried to act normal, but in my head, I was envisioning my nearest escape route and thinking how I needed to get the hell out of there. He kept going on and on, saying that I had his dead girlfriend's 'aura', and how he knew from the minute I came in that there was something special about me. Before I could say anything, he had a fistful of my hair and was stroking it, citing that my hair even felt like his dead girlfriend's hair. I yanked my head away and nervously laughed, envisioning him wearing my hair as a wig.

I finally managed to claim exhaustion and retire to my room. Before I left, he made me promise that I would come on his motorbike with him to the river in the morning. Having no plans of ending up floating with the fish in the river, I set a booby trap on my door and stayed awake all night listening for the sounds of his creepy little footsteps.

I woke up at five in the morning, left some money on the end table, and ended up sneaking out the backdoor of the guesthouse. I was legit running to the nearest bus station, jumping over bushes with my giant pack like goddamn Rambo. Thinking I was maybe being dramatic, I was still taking no chances.

I would like to say I was overreacting, but as the bus was pulling away, I saw Dead Girlfriend guy running down the street looking for me. I managed to crouch down on the bus. My last sight of him was him kicking the curb angrily.

My second notable brush with fear came in India. I was about to embark on a week-long yoga retreat in the hippie haven on the Ganges River, Rishikesh. I arranged for a driver in Delhi to drive me the seven-hour journey to Rishikesh.

I knew it would be an interesting ride after I was already in the backseat of my taxi driver's cab. I noticed my driver's eyes were extremely bloodshot and that he kept repeatedly downing some weird drink concoction.

About two hours into the swerving ride, I started to get a little frightened as I could visibly see him dozing off and returning to consciousness while barreling down the road at 80km per hour. I asked him if he was alright, but he just shrugged crankily at me. He just resumed driving, occasionally swerving into the next lane.

I rested my head on the window and resolutely decided to ignore him. This didn't work, as I was jolted awake by a large shake and crashing sound. **He had driven into another car.** Unsurprisingly, the other driver began shaking his fists in rage and following us down the freeway. Vin Diesel over here refused to stop and just upped the speed. We were barreling down the freeway like a goddamn *Fast and the Furious* chase. He ended up losing our pursuer, while I just sat dumbfounded in the back.

The rest of the ride was fairly uneventful, as the large dent in the side of his car seemed to be a wake-up call. We arrived in Rishikesh around 8pm, and it was already dark. **My driver pulled over, and a random man opened the door and hopped into the car with us.** I was immediately freaked out. I started to ask who this person was, but they just kept conversing with each other in Hindi.

I started to have a mild panic attack as we pulled out of the city center and down a dark, narrow street. The car stopped at the end of the road. I could make out a dimly lit path that led into the woods by the Ganges. They both got out of the car and pointed towards the path stating *"Ashram...that way."*

At this point, I was having a full-fledged anxiety attack. I refused to get out of the car, and without thinking, locked them both out as they looked on with bemused expressions.

Yes...I locked my driver out of his own car.

Loudly proclaiming that I wanted to go back into a well-lit area, I started shouting at them that they needed to call the ashram immediately. They kept just saying it was through the dark woods while pointing and laughing. Finally, they got the manager of the ashram on the phone, who told me that the ashram was indeed through the woods.

Half thinking that I was still going to be murdered, I got out of the car and paid the driver. About five minutes into the pitch-black walk, I saw the lights of the ashram and nearly cried with relief. Feeling quite silly for locking him out of the car, I apologized and checked into my room for the night.

So, the 'random man' did indeed work for the ashram, but it would have been nice to have an introduction. (Side note, we're homies now and have laughed about the whole 'I thought you were going to rape/mutilate/murder me' thing).

Now Kaitlyn, you're probably wondering, 'How on Earth does being scared to your wits end lend itself to fearlessness?'

Well, what doesn't kill you really does make you stronger. Dealing with sticky situations in a foreign country is scary and intimidating, but somehow-you get through it. You will discover that you are far more capable than you thought that you could possibly be. Getting around in a foreign city, not knowing anyone, and not just surviving, but *thriving*, is a skill, and you will be able to say that you have done it.

After traveling and backpacking for a while, I transitioned to more of an expat lifestyle. When I first moved to Hanoi, Vietnam, I had to learn how to drive a motorbike in rush hour. While at first this heaving mass of traffic seemed dangerous, terrifying, and impossible, driving there soon became second nature. It became as normal to me as driving a car back in Seattle. I learned to ride that moped like a true pro, swerving dogs, cats, and crates of chickens.

One day, I got stuck in a massive monsoon coming back from a bar around 11pm. It was my first month in Hanoi, so I didn't know my way around so well. I pulled into a dark, dry overhang to load Google Maps, and realized with dismay that I was out of data. If you haven't experienced a tropical rainstorm, envision howling winds, tree branches falling on the road, and rain so thick it's impossible to see through. I started to cry, and then started to laugh at the absolute absurdity of my situation. I quickly brushed off my tears when I realized there was no one that would help me out of this mess but myself. Hysteria is only possible with an audience. I set my resolve and ventured back into the torrential rainstorm, eventually making my way home

Streets of Hanoi, Vietnam

When you face your fears head on, they become much more manageable. In my travels abroad, I've done things that I never imagined possible. This sense that I really can accomplish anything lends itself well to whenever I face a challenge or think I can't do something. Traveling solo can be rough. Traveling in general is messy. It's not glamorous, it's not the front of a postcard. But, as with most difficult things in life, it's worth it.

Tam Coc, Vietnam

Compassion

The next lesson that I've taken away from my travel was one of compassion. I learned this lesson in many countries, but nothing stuck with me quite as much as my time in India.

Ah, India.

My journey through India was wrought with epic highs and lows. India is chaotic, dirty, and yet-still intoxicating. India takes no prisoners. Either you love it, or you hate it. There is no middle ground. I quickly learned that in order to survive in India, you have to be able to find peace in the midst of absolute insanity.

In India, poverty is at its most brutal. There are mansions positioned next door to slums, and government corruption is at its finest. India doesn't let you look away from the sights you would rather not see.

It teaches you-in the most painful way possible-to be grateful for the life you lead.

As humans, the best thing we can give in this world is our love and compassion to others. Everyone deserves kindness. When you open up your heart and trust in the goodness of other people, you will be rewarded. Indian people are some of the most generous and welcoming people I have ever met, and that's part of why I had such a positive experience there.

I visited northern India on one of my many backpacking trips. Jodhpur, or 'The Blue City', is by far my favorite city in Rajasthan. Sunny streets, exotic alleyways, and colorful markets make it just enthralling enough to feel almost otherworldly. Towering over the city lies Mehrangarh, a giant fort that stands about 120m above Jodhpur city. Around the fort's base, glittering streets wind around, smelling of incense, sewers, and spices.

About a two-hour bus ride from Jodhpur lies the small desert town, Osian. I didn't know this when I arrived, but Osian is a significant pilgrimage site. Sachiya Mata Temple is very popular for local worshippers. I arrived in Osian alone, and quickly realized I was the only foreigner there as I walked through the desert marketplace up to the steps of the temple. Before I knew it, a long line of people had formed behind me, all craning to get a look. One woman reached up and stroked my hair, while another band of children stood around me, laughing and daring each other to shout *'Hello!'*

I ended up waiting in the line with other pilgrims for about an hour to view the temple, which was one of the most unorganized lines I've ever seen. People began pushing on either side of me, shoving me into a gate enclosed line. At first, I was slightly on edge, as I was a woman trapped alone in a giant crowd of people. However, I was met with outstanding amounts of compassion and warmth. One woman started braiding my hair, while another reached over and touched my eyeliner.

Jodhpur, India

It was in this moment I realized how false the narrative of 'the other' was. The world isn't really as scary as news media outlets and politicians would like us to believe. After we exited the temple, I was surrounded by people, all begging to take photos. One woman posed with me while I shook her hand and smiled awkwardly, while another thrust her baby into my arms.

People in India went out of their way to show me immense amounts of kindness. While I was wandering through some back streets in India, I met a woman named Mishti. Mishti had seen that I was lost and invited me into her home for some chai. We sat around drinking hot, milky chai and henna painting. Mishti had two children, although she was only 22. She told me that she was eager to converse with foreigners because she wanted to hear different outlooks on the world. She had wished to go farther with her schooling, but priority had been given to her brother because she was a girl. Her spirit, warmth, and generosity left a lasting impact on me. Although Mishti was far from rich, she waved me off from paying for anything, citing that I was her guest.

Another family invited me to take part in their intimate celebration, singing and clapping while I bowed to Ganesh in their doorstep. India never fails to baffle me, because it is a country of extremes. It is both ugly and beautiful, kind and cruel, peaceful yet chaotic.

Traveling inevitably leads you to question the world and your place in it. I have questioned my own privilege and questioned the materialism and consumerism that is so prevalent in the United States. When you begin to see the world for what it is, and not what you have been conditioned to believe, your paradigm shifts. You will begin to question things that you thought were certain and replace your old truths with new beliefs that are founded on experience rather than the distorted perception the media gives of the world.

Most of all, I have begun to realize that no matter where you go, it's always people that make the place.

Throughout my journey, the places would have meant nothing if it wasn't for the kindness and warmth of the people that inhabit it. I have immense amounts of gratitude for the other lost travelers, the acts of generosity from strangers, and the smiles from people that will stay imprinted on my heart forever.

Hanoi, Vietnam

Presence

Above all, travel has taught me that NOW is the most important moment, and the only moment that will ever truly matter.

Travel lends itself to the traveler being present in a way that not many other things in life do. If it's done right, it feels like an endless state of flow. For most, travel is not permanent or routine, and thus you have a natural tendency to want to suck the marrow out of every experience and truly feel moments to their absolute fullest. I have many fond memories of nights under the stars on the beach, lulled to sleep by acoustic guitars and the sound of the waves. Nights spent at bars in dirty hostels, nights laughing over noodles at roadside stalls in Asia, nights running through exotic streets and feeling absolutely infinite.

As I get older, my travels have turned more introspective. I've recently moved to Bali, and it's an island of beauty and raw healing. Yoga, breath-work, ecstatic dance, meditation, you name it—I've probably been trying it. Bali is a place that heals, but it also brings things to the surface that you may have been avoiding.

Bali, Indonesia

I knew that Bali was the place I needed in my life after I attended a ceremony at a local village. Seeing everyone together-praying, chanting, and meditating, gives such an immense and beautiful sense of unity.

When I arrived on this magical island, **I knew I wanted to visit a Balinese healer.** I've had some serious issues with insomnia throughout my life, and while some of it's productive in a sense-I find myself more creative at 3am-it's not healthy. I ended up finding a Guru, and after much back & forth, he agreed to see me.

It was a soul-healing experience. You know when you meet someone and light just radiates from their very being? He was one of those people. During the treatment, I was drenched with water and meditated while he prayed. And-what do you know? I've been sleeping like a baby ever since. *Some may say this was in my head-but wasn't my original problem as well?*

Bali, Indonesia

To break through, you need to be broken open. Wounds need to be open to begin to heal. Since I've been allowing this beautiful place into my soul, I've discovered that the only place to be is here, right now.

I've been overwhelmed with this crazy gratitude for myself, for the planet, and the kind & loving souls around me.

And so, I am eternally grateful for the adventures, for the healing, and for the life I have been blessed to live.

I want to shake people sometimes. Shake some fire into them. Make them see that *"You only live once"* isn't some dumb cliché. This moment is literally all we have. The only moment that matters is now. For me, traveling was what lent itself to this realization. It opened up pathways for me that I couldn't have dreamed of before I started this journey. Sometimes, when we separate ourselves from everything we've known, it allows the way for new channels, new paradigms and new thoughts to enter our consciousness. Old habits are replaced by gratitude and joy.

I want to celebrate being madly, wildly, in love with my life. I want to sleep under the stars, swim in the sea, and live life the way it was meant to be lived-with absolute rapture. I like my life the way it is when I am traveling. *Unconstrained. Free.* And if you are like me, you probably do as well. I want to be shameless. I want to experiment. I want to be able to kiss a stranger in any corner of the world, drink an espresso in Paris, climb mountains and feel the rush of the air on my wind-chapped cheeks. I want to own moments, not investments. **I want to celebrate being madly, crazily in love with my life.**

Mui Ne, Vietnam

Society is strange...You go to school, get a job, get married, and have kids. You may have settled in your relationship, and in your career, but you're getting praise from others. You must be doing something correct. Right? You get the mortgage, the pension plan and the house, yet something is still missing.

We all have been told that life is a race, and so we are always looking to the future. We have forgotten how to be present in the moment. Life just comes and goes, and it wasn't exactly good.

But hey, it wasn't terrible, right?

In this race to the finish, we've forgotten to live. In reality, the only thing we are racing towards is death.

When most of us finally wake up from this illusion that has been created for us, it is on our deathbeds. Or maybe it is because we are ill from a disease that has been caused by living an unhappy life, a life full of self-induced stress and anxiety. We realize that we didn't accomplish our dreams. We listened to the people who scolded us and said, *"Be realistic."* We stopped evolving, growing, and learning.

Most of all, we forgot what a beautiful, magical, experience it is simply to be **alive.**

This is for those who don't want to settle. Don't feel bad about your burning desire for more. To keep quiet about this desire is one of the biggest disservices you can do to yourself. I won't feel guilty for it. I won't feel guilty for not settling on the most valuable thing in my life-my happiness. I won't feel guilty because I want more. Not everyone wants kids and a relationship and a white picket fence. I want windy bus rides to God-knows-where, fleeting longing glances on train rides, cups of chai passed to me from locals. I want to watch a sunset and applaud when it's finished because I was just lucky enough to witness a tiny miracle.

You shouldn't feel the need to be in a relationship, or have a mortgage payment, or anything else that society is shoving down your throat. Call me idealistic or whimsical or foolish but my wanderlust nature drives me forward and I can't, nor do I want to stop it. My heart longs for things I don't even know yet, things I haven't even experienced yet. *Something in me wants more.*

I'm not sorry. And you shouldn't be either. xx

Kaitlyn Knoll

My name is Kaitlyn and I'm a 20-something who has a passion for backpacking solo. I love sharing my own crazy adventures and inspiring other travelers to pursue their passions and dreams. Nothing makes me happier then when like-minded people learn to embrace their restless spirits and wandering feet.

Instagram: kaitlynknoll
Website: www.wayfarerkate.com

No Hurry to Get Home

by Daniela Ramos

The Unfortunate Beginning

October 2, 2013 was the day I woke up only to find my life was about to fall apart. My biggest worry that morning was a university history paper that was due the following day, but somehow, twelve hours later, I left university and New York City for good.

At least I didn't have to finish that boring essay anymore.

I won't go into details on how it all happened because it seems like history now. It was all due to a lack of planning on my part, and the delusion that the whole world was at my feet without wanting to put much effort into making things happen for myself. I was just a lost 18-year-old who wasn't ready for life.

That same night, I booked a flight to Mexico City with the last $200 I had to my name. I needed to be around people who loved me, and I needed time to recollect my feelings before attempting to take any further steps at putting my life back together.

University was never something I wanted to pursue. When I was eleven, I told my father I would never finish school and I would instead travel the world taking pictures.

In spite of that dream, I grew up, and growing up means forgetting what really matters. I grew up and began thinking the things I needed were the things everyone else had and I began turning into the person I thought others would accept.

I saved my own money throughout the following months and thanks to the help of many people, I was on my way to London a few months later to study a three-month-long course in the heart of Soho. I didn't have enough money for accommodation, but I knew I had to do it. Instead of renting a flat, I couch surfed, moving every 3-4 days to a new home. During these months, I met some of the most amazing characters - first was Stuart, a guy who ended up putting me up for a month and is still to date one of my best friends. After he finished his master's degree, he worked for one of the most prestigious architecture companies in London only to ditch it a year later and travel the world. Then there was Tom, who hosted me in an expensive apartment overlooking the London Eye. Next was Jane, an American girl who was working for Apple, followed by Anne, a Mexican girl who was living with a dodgy fashion photographer in Hackney.

I've forgotten most of what I learned during the course, but through the stories of the people who hosted me, I learned how possible travel was. I learned that hitchhiking wasn't synonymous to getting murdered, I'd always meet kind-hearted people wherever I went, and that I did not have to stick to the norms of society and I could choose my own path.

Prague, Czechia

On weekends, I would fly to far-off places; it was cheaper to go to Eastern Europe than to stay in the city. I went to Düsseldorf to celebrate Carnival, I strolled the alleys of Prague, and I fell in love with Zagreb.

Traveling didn't cost a fortune after all.

Three months later, my stay in London was over. I flew back to Mexico feeling utterly lost again, and much to my unhappiness, I enrolled back into university and got an internship at my uncle's company.

London had spoiled me. I suddenly had the terrifying realization that I was going through the motions of life without really feeling any of it. Normal didn't suit me anymore after having seen a part of the world. I wanted to see it all. I began hosting couchsurfers at home and would gorge myself on their travel stories.

I wanted to do the same thing they were doing, I craved the road.

I spent the next few months freelancing and saving every single cent I could with the idea of booking a flight to Europe and never looking back.

A few months later, I nervously stepped into the airport, checked in my backpack at the counter, and flew to Madrid on a one-way with just $1000 to my name.

It wasn't easy, but I made it work. After three months of wayward restlessness, things got dark. The money was running out, the temperatures were quickly decreasing, and I began thinking it had all been a terrible idea. Petrol stations and bus terminals became my home and my main mode of transport was hitching lifts from strangers by the road.

How could I ever think that I, of all people, could pull something like this off? What I really wanted to do then was go home and cry.

I made it to Croatia in October. Throughout the previous months, I had managed to earn a bit of money freelancing online, but at this point my bank account was quickly emptying.

Between the summer and fall of 2015, the refugee influx that struck Europe was at its peak. The war that hit Syria was giving its citizens no choice than to flee to nearby countries. At the time I found myself in Croatia, orders were given to Slovenia to block its borders, leaving thousands of people stuck in refugee camps.

I resolved to spend a few weeks in one of the border camps to help out. Every day for a week, I'd head there to give out clothes to newcomers, most of which were given to the camp by two crazy Germans who had been driving back and forth in a van from Germany with donated clothes they collected.

It was a few weeks later that an opportunity in Thailand arose. I had been applying to several work exchange jobs around the world in the hopes that I could trading work for accommodation. My plan then was to spend the next three months working online to rebuild my funds and continue on to backpack in Papua New Guinea.

It didn't work out. Thailand called and I was offered a job that would have me traveling through two continents collecting stories and memories through written pieces and photographs. Life had its own plans for me then.

Over the following year I traveled almost non-stop for the job and began coming up with my own aspirations. As much as I loved the opportunity to get paid to travel, I began yearning for my own plans and the freedom to go wherever I wanted. Through rediscovered passions, a pretty fearless attitude that travel had inflicted upon me, and the endless amount of inspirational ideas that every new town or village I set foot in gave me, I began creating my own projects that now allow me to hop on the next flight to…well, wherever I want.

Chiang Mai, Thailand

Hitchhiking in Ireland and Sleeping Inside Castle Ruins

The story of how my mother's side of the family ended up in Mexico is long-winded and meant for another day, but I was incredibly excited to visit the area my ancestors had once called their home.

The Donegal county in the north of Ireland boasts an almost non-existent public transportation system, so I decided hitchhiking would do the trick. I made my way up to Belfast, where I met adventure-hungry travelers, Karolina and Stephen, who decided to join the escapade. With only $200 left to my name, I told them I had been toying with the idea of sleeping inside a few abandoned castles I'd been researching in a book, to which they eagerly agreed.

The following day we were on our way to Raphoe, the home of the first castle I had mapped out.

Standing on the roadside, we decided to split up into two groups of two to increase our chances of somebody having space in their car to give us a lift. Whoever made it to Raphoe first would wait for the others.

Less than five minutes later, a man in a BMW drove by and stopped to pick us up. "Where are you headed?" he asked. "Raphoe," we replied. "I can get you close to there, but you'll need to find another lift after the junction."

He drove past Karolina and Stephen and asked if they were our friends and told us to tell them to hop in. "That was smart of you guys, splitting up to get a better chance to catch a ride. I used to hitch a lot when I was younger," he said proudly. He told us the craziest tales of the years he spent traveling Europe. "But look at me now!" he stated. "I own a successful company, but man, I sure do miss those carelessly free times."

He drove past the junction we were originally supposed to get off at without saying a word. We all looked at each other in confusion before he told us he was driving us all the way to Raphoe.

It was nine in the evening when we began climbing our way up towards the castle at the edge of town. Now left in ruins and set inside a farm, the castle was built during the 17th-century and destroyed by an accidental fire almost two centuries ago after surviving several attacks.

We hesitated at the realization that the castle wasn't completely abandoned and instead was located inside a farm, but we leaped over the fence and on to private property anyway as the idea was too engraved in our heads at this point.

We set our sleeping bags under the only room that was left with a roof as Karolina shouted "Are we really doing this?! It's insane, I don't think I'll be able to sleep at all!"

As the sun began setting, we noticed six cows peeking into our self-proclaimed abode's hatch, wondering what we were doing there. They disappeared after a few minutes, as though they were telling us they wouldn't warn the owners of the farm about our unsolicited presence.

A Month in a Monastery School in Myanmar

It was sort of unplanned how I winded up teaching geography at a monastery school in the Nanshe district of the city of Mandalay. I originally headed there for a project I was assigned - I was meant to stay there a few days, take a few photos and document my experiences, but it soon became much more than that.

Exploring the markets of Nanshe, Mandalay, Myanmar

The school was founded more than two decades ago and quickly grew into a free education facility for thousands of students and the home to many young Burmese who traveled from far-off villages in order to be able to go to school. Most of the students residing there adopted a monastic lifestyle.

While here, I met Mary, an Italian girl my age who was volunteering as an English teacher and we quickly became partners in crime. It wasn't long until a few of the curious novice monks began talking to us whenever we walked through the school during the evenings.

First came Tony, a bright-eyed 19-year-old novice who approached us and introduced himself in broken English. After three days, I shyly confessed to him that I couldn't remember his name.

"Toninual," he said.

"Huh?"

"Tooon-niii-nual," he repeated.

No matter how many times I tried pronouncing it, I simply couldn't, so I asked him if it would be all right for me to call him "Tony."

Very soon after, his friends joined in and we became a sort of "gang" who hung out together every day. They all asked us to give them nicknames, and we tried to match them as best as we could with their real names.

They'd often take us on stints around the city, showing us the hidden sides of Mandalay guidebooks don't tell you about. We'd hop from temple to temple in an attempt to learn as much as we could about Buddhism and life in Mandalay. In return, the novice monks would ask us to teach them English.

One day, Tim and Andre, two of the students we had befriended, approached and asked me if I could give them a geography class after school. I'd spend hours at the school library gorging on the donated books about the world and they'd often asked me why I was so interested in the faraway lands, whenever they found me reading a book on the crumbling wooden bench next to my room. I couldn't help but tell them that seeing the world was my greatest passion, but understanding it was just as important and I was intent on getting to know every corner of it.

I'd teach them geography when I could, usually past ten in the evening after they'd finished their normal classes and homework, and I was astonished at how many students attended without hesitation.

I had to laugh whenever I realized what was happening. I used to read about Buddhism and monks in my geography books when I was at school, but I never imagined that one day I'd be hanging out with a group of them like it was nothing.

One afternoon, rain began pouring and flooded the entire school. The students tucked the lower parts of their robes into their waist and turned them into a sort of shorts and began playing football inside a giant puddle under the rain. Two other foreigners I'd met at the school and I took our flipflops off and jumped in to join the game. I was completely soaked and my skills were less than ideal, but all I could do was grin as I attempted to kick the ball that would quickly disappear from my sight as I realized how insanely beautiful my life was at that moment.

A month later, I left the school. My train to Yangon was set to leave in the afternoon and I couldn't help but cry when Tony chased me down and hugged me goodbye in the middle of the bustling street in front of the school.

Monks are not allowed to hug women, but he did it anyway.

Spending a Week in a Maasai Village

My legs were numb as the public jeep packed with at least a dozen people and two goats turned left from the paved highway and began winding its way through the savanna.

While the car was full, that didn't seem to stop more passengers from hopping on to get a ride. There was still room left on the roof, after all.

My next destination after four incredible months of traveling through eastern Africa was an authentic Maasai village in the middle of nowhere. I was going to be hosted by Kimani, a Maasai man I had met in Arusha through my work.

As we got deeper into the wild bushes of Tanzania, Kimani took out a vibrant red Shuka and wrapped it around himself. "I have to dress like this whenever I go to my village," he announced.

Two hours later, we arrived in Amloret, a village so tiny and secluded from the outside world that the only concrete buildings within it were a small clinic, a church, and a school. Everything else was mud houses that the villagers called home.

And then there was my home for the week, a house in the village where Kimani had arranged for me to stay with a local family. It was probably the most well-equipped dwelling in the area, but it still lacked showers and a toilet, which was really nothing more than a hole in the ground inside a hut.

I went on long walks every day, spotting grazing giraffes and impalas along the way. During my time in Amloret, the river had completely dried up and the Maasai women residing there were in charge of walking kilometers on end with their donkeys to fetch water from a borehole. They'd all gather there, filling their buckets with water while giggling and gossiping, wearing the latest in chromatic and vivid clothing that added colors to the neutral palette that made up the landscape.

Northern Tanzania

I'd also run into Maasai men grazing their cattle inside the forest. At the time, most of the males in the village were occupied digging seeps to reach the water underground for their cattle to drink.

In the late afternoons, everyone would head back home, where the villagers loved to fill my mind with stories of the times they fought against lions who would come on to their property to eat their cattle. I remained at the edge of my seat, eating up their stories as though they were a feast.

One morning, while on my usual walk, I spotted a Maasai warrior walking in my direction on the savanna. When we finally crossed paths, he bowed his head and I did the same. He was incredibly shy and barely spoke any English, but we managed to have a small conversation before I asked permission to photograph him.

It's hard to pinpoint exactly what made my time in Amloret so special, but there was something about it that has forever stuck with me. The serenity in which he walked and his eyes that were set wide apart from each other, stared at me with an intensity that made my knees feel weak.

A Maasai man and his cattle, Northern Tanzania

That Time I Was Confused for a Drug Mule in the Middle East

Three long-winded layovers and forty-eight hours of travel time after leaving Europe, I finally made it to the Middle East.

My plans to arrive swiftly into the Jordanian capital and head over to a warm, cozy bed were cut short after the immigration officer looked at my passport with suspicion.

"Something wrong?" I enquired.

"Are you traveling alone?" he asked.

"Yes."

"Do you have a husband?"

"A boyfriend."

"Why is he not here with you?"

"He is busy with school right now."

"Why did he allow you to come alone?"

"Umm..."

"Please follow us", said two men that were not dressed like immigration officers at all.

"Why?" I asked nervously. These men did not look official at all, neither one of them was wearing uniforms.

"Is someone waiting for you outside the airport?"

I didn't want to answer, I didn't want for them to know that I didn't know a single soul in the country and no one around was waiting for me to show up.

I grabbed my phone to text my boyfriend what was happening, just in case I was about to go missing, but before I even managed to type in half the message, they snatched it away from my hands.

"You are not allowed to communicate with anyone until we are finished," they exclaimed angrily as they began pulling me towards a small room.

"Please tell me what is going on and where you are taking me," I pleaded, with tears filling my eyes.

"We believe you are carrying drugs."

Silence

"Daniela, it is better if you tell us now. We are about to check every part of your body and luggage and if we find anything, you will be in big trouble."

Every part of your body. What a perfect way to word it. This is when I completely lost it.

Scenes of these men touching my body to "search for drugs" in that dark room we were about to enter flashed before me.

If their intention really was to confirm I was not a drug trafficker... what if - someone, somehow - had placed drugs in my checked luggage?

I wasn't sure which option was worse. My fate was written, and it wasn't pretty.

We entered the room to find a fat, Arab man sitting on his desk – he was their boss. Cigarette smoke circled around the room and made its way up to the roof. I was asked to take a seat. A tall woman was sitting in the opposite corner.

The sight of another lady calmed me. Maybe they did just want to make sure I was clear, and everything would be ok.

As his assistant lit up a cigarette, I asked if I could smoke one as well. They allowed it. "Daniela, we have a reason to believe you are trafficking illegal drugs into Jordan."

"Why? Because I am Mexican?"

"Yes. And you were pretty nervous when my colleagues were bringing you here."

I flipped out and told him, yes, of course, I was nervous. Two random men who did not look at all official began dragging me into a room, telling me my body would be searched and asking questions to see if I was on my own.

Was I wrong to assume that, just because Jordan is a country with a Muslim majority, the men had bad intentions?

Probably, but I do still think the whole situation was handled incorrectly by them. He seemed to disregard my answer and continued on to ask for his assistant to open my luggage.

He proceeded to rummage through my suitcase as thoroughly as possible. Also, it doesn't really help when half of your products' ingredients are written in Thai.

Did I mention I am a very messy packer? The look on his face gave me the clue me that he was wondering if a 5-year-old had packed for me.

And nothing was found.

They had a look at my passport and found my Yellow Fever Vaccine certificate, which they stared at for a good five minutes, puzzled.

"What is this?"

"It's a certificate for my vaccinations?"

"What?"

"You know, when they put medicine through a needle," I replied proudly. That was a dumb way to word it.

"DRUGS???!!!!"

"No! It is for my health, to stop a disease when I go to Africa."

"AIDS?!"

Suddenly, I was this AIDS-ridden Mexican drug trafficker.

"No, no. It is a normal procedure. Everyone gets it," I lied, "You can Google it."

Next up was a body check. I told him I would not allow for a man to do the check and he appointed the mysterious woman sitting in the corner to do so. We entered another small room, and, while I undressed, I felt the stinky smell of my two-day-old socks creeping in.

How embarrassing.

You know for sure you are not trafficking drugs when you are being searched by a Middle Eastern government and your biggest worry is how much your feet stink.

She let me out and I lit another cigarette, this time much more relaxed than before.

Until they asked me for my phone's password. Oh, god.

They began searching through my Whatsapp messages, desperately trying to prove that I was indeed in Jordan for the wrong reasons.

They could have found misleading messages. You see, I have a pretty aloof sense of humor and I don't mind making fun of myself. When my friends joke about me selling drugs, (because I am Mexican and they can't think of a more original way to mock me), I will joke about it back.

It's all fun and games until you actually become a suspect.

I must have chain-smoked at least ten cigarettes during the half an hour they were reading through my messages. To my luck, however, they stopped right before my latest joke about bringing drugs into Europe from Thailand began.

They apologized for making wrong assumptions based on nationality and the following half an hour was spent talking about Jordan, the attractions I shouldn't miss during my time there and so on.

I was dismissed and as I walked out the door, he told me "Before I forget: You can buy cigarettes on the first floor here at the airport. I think after this experience you need to smoke at least ten more."

Yes, I do.

Petra, Jordan
Four Years Later

Life is funny, really.

Had things gone the way I had planned back in 2013, I would have just graduated university and would likely be looking desperately for a job in the city, always pushing travel back, always putting aside the things my heart was desperately craving.

I wish I would have known that things were being taken away from me in order to give space to the life I was meant to lead. Had things gone the way I planned, I would have never spent a year living in a tiny riverside village in Thailand, I wouldn't have hitchhiked my way through Europe, or spent a week living in a Maasai village in the wild bushes of Tanzania. I would have never crossed 13,000 kilometers of the African continent using solely public transport while collecting the wildest of stories along the way.

Today, I am the happiest I have ever been. Travel shaped my career in so many ways and made me rediscover passions I had concealed deep within. Travel revealed to me the things I had wanted to do for a long time and gave me inspiration for new ambitions - all of which I pursued and have allowed me to continue this weird and wonderful life trotting the world.

Whatever it is you want is awaiting you on the other side of fear.

Daniela Ramos

Three years after taking the plunge and booking a one-way ticket to Madrid to travel the world indefinitely, Daniela returned to Mexico City to explore her own roots and start her travel blog, No Hurry To Get Home. Daniela created a life of travel by becoming a photographer, a graphic designer, and a content creator for both her own blog as well as several other online publications. Moreover, two years into her travels, she started Nomadik Market, an online shop that sells slow fashion and handcrafted home decoration created by female artisans from Latin America and Africa.

She currently splits her time between Mexico and Germany, but you'll more often than not find her gallivanting around the world, either revisiting old places she loved or discovering new destinations.

Blog: www.nohurrytogethome.com
Store: www.nomadikmarket.com

Silent Witness

by Jennifer Armstrong

I did not discover travel until I had finished university and moved from my small town to a neighbouring big city. I had a very sheltered childhood and grew up without any sense of the vastness of the world. It was not until I met my partner that I was introduced to the many histories, civilizations and countries that were woven into the fabric of humanity. After several trips around the globe together, from Europe to Asia to Africa, my desire to explore became insatiable. I learned the basics of navigation and grew comfortable with the routines involved with travel so that I was somewhat confident to journey on my own. I embarked on numerous solo journeys, often visiting many countries per trip and leaving for months at a time to discover what else I had been missing for the first two decades of my life.

My difficulty with travel is that I have always been a very shy individual. To speak to strangers was an impossibility in my youth, and this was the most difficult challenge to surmount when traveling alone. I tried to be prepared for anything prior to traveling simply to reduce the chance I would need to ask someone for help. So I prepared my flights, accommodations, itinerary and maps in great detail. I wanted to be ready for anything that might arise so that I could navigate my way from city to city and country to country without issue. Most importantly, I did not want to find myself in a situation where I would need to ask anyone for help.

Journey to Croatia

Colosseum of Pula

One summer, I decided to explore Croatia. I had explored much of Western Europe and was enthralled by the images of the nature in Croatia, so I chose this country to introduce me to Central Europe. I had heard about a new type of accommodation called Airbnb and decided to try it for the first time. I had many reservations about using Airbnb – what if my host or other travelers in the same apartment stole from me while I was out? Or if they were loud and kept me awake? How would I even find the place without a sign out front? Would there be someone available for me to ask questions, or book me a cab, similar to the front desk staff of a hotel? My research assured me that if I reserved a place with good reviews, I would be fine.

My first stop would be a small city in the western part of the country. I arrived at the airport in Pula at 11:00 p.m. I pointed to the address on my reservation when I got into a cab, and the driver promptly dropped me off in front of a nondescript building. I had strong doubts that this was where I was supposed to be. I knocked, but no answer. The metal door looked more like a gate to keep people out rather than an entryway to a living space. I called the number on my reservation, and the lady's voice assured me she would be right down to let me in.

The woman was curt. She showed me my room, pointed to her room across the hall where she would retreat not to be seen again, and said there would be two more travelers arriving soon to stay in the room next to mine. She vanished before I had any time to gather my thoughts or make any inquiries, and I knew that I would be on my own.

After a few days exploring the town, I planned to depart by bus to Zagreb. I tried to find my host to clarify where the bus station was, but I did not want to disturb her behind her closed bedroom door. I also mapped the bus station with GPS on my phone and decided I would find it on my own. I departed early and allowed myself extra time to walk what should be a 30-minute walk according to my directions. Once I arrived at the point where my GPS had directed me, I suddenly realized I was at a bus maintenance building and there was no bus station in sight! I asked the mechanics where the bus station was, but no one spoke English. Desperately, I showed them my bus ticket, and someone gestured in a certain direction and I believed he said it was a 10-20 minute walk. I took off in that direction, doubting that I was headed the right way as I jogged next to a freeway. After waving my arms in an attempt to find a cab (clearly this was not a country where it is custom to flag down a cab), I diverted to side streets. I came upon two women and begged them to point me to the bus station. They also did not speak English but pointed me in a different direction than the last man. I decided to follow the new direction, and from a distance, could make out a bus terminal ahead. As I got closer, I realized I was on the wrong side of the fence from where I needed to board the bus. My watch indicated five minutes until departure, and I was painfully aware that this was the only bus of the day leaving for Zagreb and that to miss it would cause a cascade effect on my travel plans as I would miss further activities and transportation that I had already planned. I turned to nearby construction workers and frantically asked them which way I should go to get to the bus. They laughed at me, sweat dripping down my face and a 25 lb. backpack weighing me down. I looked at them incredulously, trying to find humour in what I must look like, and trying not to feel hurt. One of the men pointed to the right, and off I took. I was the last one to board the bus, and the driver had already closed the undercarriage where luggage was stored. My backpack would not fit on my lap or beneath my feet for the four-hour drive, so the driver threw it to the ground by the exit where it remained for the trip. I was thirsty, hot, and shaking with anxiety. I realized that my timidity had made me avoid asking someone for clarity before I had left Pula. I was angry at myself for not finding the courage to simply *ask* someone.

Zagreb to Pag

When I arrived in Zagreb, I stayed at my first hostel. I avoided the common areas so as not to be confronted with an awkward social situation that I could not navigate because of its newness to me. I asked desk staff to indicate where the shuttle bus was and made my way to Plitvice Lakes National Park for a day trip.

It was cram packed with tourists. I wandered the wooden pathways and suspended canopies through the forest and came upon many waterfalls. The water was so clear I could see schools of fish swimming just below the surface. I was disappointed that swimming was not permitted, but could understand why the country sought to preserve this scene of bright blue water and wildlife. After a full day of exploring, I made my way to an island called Pag.

In Pag, I had reserved an apartment run by an elderly couple. This made for a nice change of environment from the youth hostel the night before. The beach quickly turned into party central – with clubs opening and attractive girls giving free drink tickets to people lounging on the rocky shore. I planned to escape before

I had to face an onslaught of drunken party-goers, but as I made my way from the sea I decided to turn in a ticket that I received from a club promoter and claim a free drink. I had not met anyone on this trip, so thought I'd see what comes of it when I place myself into a social space. There was a pool in the centre of the club, and many bikini-clad women and topless men were dancing without a care, splashing everyone they could reach. I decided to be honest with myself – I was out of place and stood in a corner while I quietly finished my drink. I made my way back to my apartment and realized I was quickly becoming ill. Not the kind of ill from too much drinking – but something else. I was stumbling and using every bit of effort I could muster to stay conscious and follow the street back to my apartment. The elderly couple asked if I had a good day, to which I replied with a nod before scurrying to my room. I looked at the clock which read 6:00 p.m. and laid down.

Plitvice Lakes National Park, Croatia

The next thing I remember, the sun was blazing in, and it was noon of the next day. I looked around my room and realized I was still in my bathing suit and sundress from the day before. I was completely unconscious for 18 hours and did not understand why. Disoriented, and scared that I had lost so much time, I decided to leave. I did not feel that I had anything more to gain by being in this town. The elderly man offered to drive me to the bus station, which was incredibly kind of him. He would not accept money I tried to give as a token of gratitude. I left the island with mixed feelings: a distaste for the party atmosphere, and an appreciation for the kindness of strangers who did not expect anything in return.

Zadar at Night

Before I left for my trip, I read about the Sea Organ in Zadar which was next on my itinerary. Upon arriving in the town, I quickly found it and saw that it was a series of hollow steps that descended into the water. The steps were carved in such a way that the waves would make sounds of different pitches as they crashed into them. It was an eerie echoing sound which did not seem to fit with the bright sun and happy groups of people.

Eager to see more nature, Krka National Park offered stunning waterfalls and perfectly clear water in which tourists were permitted to swim. There were fish everywhere brushing up against me as I fought the current. After three blissful hours, I wandered back to town. That evening, I saw flashing lights and heard the echo of loud music from afar and decided to find the source. I mustered up the courage to go out and explore after dark. I was restless with my many evenings alone, and although the greater part of me did not want to meet strangers, the ache of solitude drove me out into the night. I came upon something that I later learned was a "white night party" – in that the attire of the attendees was white which glowed under the black light. True to form, I was wearing black (I only travel with black clothes for simplicity: so all my garments match each other) and I was refused entry. I saw a few other people sneak through a part of the gate that was not bound together and I decided to follow them. Once inside, I walked through the crowds and observed the drinking and dancing of youth to which I could not relate. I told myself I would not be having a drink here, and opted to be a silent witness to the crowds. I did not find my time here to be terribly entertaining, but it was rather a challenge to myself to be alone amidst the various social groups. I walked through the crowd aimlessly but with a purpose, and after exploring the limits of the venue and watching the interactions of groups of friends and strangers, I grew tired and returned to my room early.

Inspired

Krka National Park, Croatia

Summit of Split

My journey continued with a bus ride to the old town of Šibenik which offered cool retreats from the heat in the form of clay churches. Exploring art and architecture in each city offers a glimpse into the culture and history of the town, and these are my favourite pastimes. I explored another antiquated town called Trogir which was home to a seaside fortress, quaint shops with local artisans, and galleries. I spent a considerable amount of time in one particular church that held many reliquaries – pieces of actual bodies of saints that were preserved in gold and glass. How strangely macabre religion can be. I find these artifacts to be a somber reminder of mortality, and one that makes me all the more determined to explore and *live*.

When I reached the aptly named city of Split, I knew I was halfway down the length of the country. This would be my base to explore some of the many ruins in the city. One day I happened upon an old Jewish cemetery on a steep hill. After climbing to the top, I found a pathway that led further, and although the path was not on my map, I was curious where it might lead. I followed the winding trail for an hour before I reached the summit. There was no one in sight as I approached the peak. I looked down and beheld the view of Split - terracotta rooftops; crumbling ruins from another century; iridescent blue water with specks of white that indicated sailboats. I savoured the moment and spun around to take in the panorama. I noticed the cliff behind me had the facade of a building carved into its surface. I managed to climb some rocks, and leaning precariously from a ledge, I peered through the metal bars that seemed to be a window. It looked like the entryway to a church but was firmly sealed. As it began to rain I started my descent, disappointed that I could not get inside. While pondering the origin of this cliffside monument I recognized the feeling of accomplishment within me, though I could not articulate exactly what I had achieved.

An Exchange of Stories

I left the city to explore an area called Makarska which reminded me of cottage country back home in Canada: dense forests; cabins on the water; docks; birds. I checked into a hostel and realized I was one of two people who were there alone: the rest of the hostel was overtaken by a group of about 20 people traveling together on a tour. It was the group's final day together and they held a party in the common room that night. I was not pleased that my room shared a wall with the common room as it was clear I would not be able to sleep until the party was over.

The other lone person staying in the hostel quickly identified that I too did not belong to the tour group. He approached me as he likewise could not sleep. He looked like a boy, but in reality he was just a few years younger than me. He told me of his aimless travels on motorcycle through Croatia, Montenegro, Armenia, Kosovo and Macedonia. He ran out of gas somewhere in Armenia and slept under a tree with his inoperable bike. He walked with it for a day, hoping to find someone who could offer him a drink of water or some gas. A farmer found him and gave him dinner and a place to sleep in spite of no shared language between them. The next day the man brought him a container of gas, and off he went to continue his journey. He was planning to go to Bosnia tomorrow on his motorcycle, and possibly explore Mostar and Sarajevo - if that was where the wind took him. He gave me an imploring look. "Come with me. When was the last time you did something spontaneous?" I did not seriously consider his offer. We had just met; I had no desire to ever ride a motorcycle; and I was planning to go to Dubrovnik tomorrow - the city I most wanted to see on this trip. But I let my mind toy with the idea for a moment. "No, I am not a risk taker," I said simply, and we shared stories for the rest of the night.

Walls of Dubrovnik

I arose after only 4 hours of sleep to catch a bus to Dubrovnik the next morning. I had reserved an Airbnb in the centre of the old city by the thick stone walls that surrounded it. There were many cobblestone steps that led down into the city, giving the feeling that I was descending into another realm - one that could perhaps be the setting of the many fantasy books I had read in childhood.

I arrived at what I was sure was the correct place, but no one answered my knock. I phoned the owner, and she said her property manager would be there momentarily. I saw a drunk man with greasy hair stumbling as he approaches and he answered his phone. I quickly pieced together that he was the manager who was supposed to let me in, and the woman I had called was now on the phone with him. She was unimpressed with the fact that he was late. The man proceeded to yell at me for getting him into trouble with his boss! I did not respond. He let me in and said the room was not ready – I could sit in the living room and wait while he cleaned it. I said I'd prefer if I could just leave my bags and get the key, so I can return later, as I was eager to explore the city. He adamantly refused and said I must sit and wait. He turned on a movie in an attempt to preoccupy me and went upstairs to clean. I was very annoyed. Half an hour later, he said my room was ready. But he could see my annoyance. He said he would only give me the keys if I drank a shot of local honey liquor. I sensed that he offered this to pacify me and salvage his reputation. I replied that no, I was exhausted and dehydrated and did not want a drink right then. He then refused to give me the key unless I drank the shot. I was angry that I was losing time that I'd rather spend exploring, so swallowed the drink, grabbed the key, and left.

I walked the walls surrounding Dubrovnik. In spite of the heat and my sheer exhaustion, it was a sublime experience. I took in the sights of the many different buildings and streets below, and at one point was overlooking the main dock with small boats and people enjoying coffee and dinner by the sea. I sat on the old stone wall, feeling accomplished that I had thoroughly explored many parts of this country. But something was unsettling me. The boy in the hostel last night – his stories of neighboring countries piqued my imagination. And his comment on my lack of spontaneity lingered on my mind. I pulled out my map of the city and saw to the northeast was Bosnia and Herzegovina, and to the southeast was Montenegro. Though I did not know much about these countries, I resolved to make my way there and see what I could learn.

View of Dubrovnik from the Walls

Stories of New Lands

After I had my fill of Dubrovnik, I took a bus to cross the Bosnian border. I found it strange that they did not even check my passport. I remembered that my grandmother had mentioned Medugorje - a city on the map that my eyes happened to land on. I recalled that she told me about a miracle there, where the Virgin Mary appeared to a group of children a few years before I was born, and she had always wanted to make the pilgrimage. I decided to see the city that she so badly wanted to visit.

Entering the country, evidence of the war some 25 years earlier was brutally obvious. The landscape reminded me of my brief foray into northern Africa. Half-built shacks of cement and stucco sparsely populated the roadside. Bus stops were not indicated by any sign, and I wondered how I, along with the few backpackers who boarded the bus, would make our way around. Upon arriving to the city, I saw that it was barren. A modern-looking church with a very tall tower marked the centre of the city and I was surprised that there was Mass occurring with what looked like at least one thousand people inside. The streets outside the church were all selling crosses, rosaries, and books about the so-called miracle.

I read a short book about the miracle while standing in a slightly air-conditioned bookshop. It told of four children who were playing on a hillside when they claimed the Virgin appeared to them at six o'clock in the evening. The next day they returned with two younger children who also bore witness to the apparition occurring at the same hour. The mass hysteria of the large number of people affected by this supposed miracle enthralled me. Upon learning about the history of this country during that period, I could see why they so desperately wanted to believe in a miracle. But the far-reaching mania of this alleged miracle over several decades and its power to transform a whole city into a major Christian tourist trap was disheartening. The book I read showed photos and biographies of the children who are now middle-aged. "Our Lady visits her daily," and, "The Virgin appears to him once a year on Christmas," ended each account. It seemed the only type of business in this town was selling overpriced plastic crosses and rosaries. I briefly questioned my faith in humanity when I saw the endless streets of shameless vendors capitalizing off of selling religious memorabilia to hordes of pilgrims and tourists.

 I quickly moved on to a nearby city called Mostar. I must admit my knowledge of the war-torn history of this city was lacking prior to my visit. It was a five-minute video in a tourist book shop that showed me the Stari Most Bridge collapse. The bridge had lasted for nearly five centuries and was destroyed by missile fire, along with the lives of many civilians. The new bridge was finished not long ago. The historians of the city say that the enemy troops were not just trying to destroy a bridge, but they were destroying memory. The memory and story of the architect who built the bridge for a sultan were ingrained into the local history of the people for generations. Destroy a structure that represents a culture, and you have destroyed the spirit of the people.

Listening to this history and seeing the old video footage of the war and the bodies of casualties made it all too real in my mind. I overheard a tour guide tell a story similar to Romeo and Juliet about a boy and girl who were in love at the time of the war, but they were from different cultural groups and their union was not accepted. They tried to escape the city together and both were shot as they ran. One died immediately and the other crawled to her lover as she died. Their bodies remained in the "no man's land" that lay between the conflicting groups. It was weeks before their families were able to lay them to rest. Their story is but one of many tragedies of this country and I tried to honour their memory as I walked the same streets they once did.

Stari Most Bridge, Mostar, Bosnia

I walked over the "new old bridge" as they called it, from the Catholic to Muslim sides. The river divided the two sides of the town. The city centre was quaint, with three ethnic groups living together in relative harmony, yet strongly identifying with their respective background. I overheard a tour guide explaining the difference between the Croats, the Serbs, and the Slovenes. As an outsider, I did not note any physical features that distinguished the three groups; only the headscarf, burka, or lack thereof gave it away. It was fascinating to learn about the history that was so recent as to have occurred when I was alive, yet which was completely unknown to me.

I sat below the busy bridge and dug my fingers into the pebbly beach. These very rocks could be the stones in the original bridge carved by the masons five centuries ago, returned back to earth. Those workers remain nameless and long gone, and I marvel at the thought that some of the locals around me could very well be related to the people of this same town so many centuries ago.

View from Stari Most Bridge

Montenegro

I had chosen a town called Budva in the relatively unknown country of Montenegro to be my next destination to explore. This town was also destroyed by war. I learned that about 90% of property here was purchased by Russians after the economic crisis some years ago. I felt like a complete foreigner – I only saw Russians with their multi-million-dollar yachts, and no other tourists. I felt their gaze as I walked by. I tried to ignore the feeling of unwelcome as I explored the winding streets. I laughed to myself upon seeing a street vendor selling thick woolen coats in the extreme heat before I remembered that the people here would be returning to a cold country when their vacation was over. The eerie quiet of this town was both intriguing and unsettling. I picked another point on the map which I hoped would be more promising and made my way to Kotor Bay.

Kotor Bay, Montenegro

Kotor was a much livelier town, although overridden with tourists from cruise ships. I saw a church in the middle of a lake, and learned it was aptly named Our

Lady of the Rocks. I took a water taxi over and gained a view of the mountains behind the stone fort that encompassed the old part of town. The church itself was on an artificial islet. I overheard the myth of its origin: the islet was supposedly made by grateful sailors who threw rocks into the lake upon returning safely from sea. It was an act of an ancient oath meant to honour the place where an image of Madonna and Child was said to have been seen beneath the surface of the sea many years ago. Again, I was in awe at the power of myth. The church charged an entrance fee to sit inside its small enclave. I found this appalling and refused to pay out of principle. Places of worship that charge for entry seem more like places of corruption or tourist traps. I try to be sympathetic to people facing economic issues as I realize that perhaps charging fees for entry or selling religious memorabilia is their only means of income, but I cannot help but feel uncomfortable when a building or site of some deep significance is used for profit in such a shameless way.

Our Lady of the Rocks Church, Montenegro

Reflections

As I took a late bus back to Croatia, I reflected on my journey. I knew that my trip was drawing to an end and flipped through the notes I had taken in my journal. As I browsed its pages, I saw that I had grown more confident as time went on. I skimmed through my photos and recalled the stunning sights of nature and architecture to which I bore witness. How foreign the landscapes and buildings were to my eyes which were previously only accustomed to the skyscrapers and traffic of a big city! I felt a pang of regret knowing I would have to return to home, but tried to remain positive that I had gained so much from this trip.

I returned to Dubrovnik as it was the nearest city with an international airport. On my final night in the city, I sat on a patio and looked out at all the people passing me by. I imagined the lives they might be living. I picture their futures: I see a young girl walking while holding her parents' hands. I envision her teen years as she tries to find herself, struggles to learn English and leave this country, find love and have her heart broken, find a modest career and establish her life in another country, and finally settle down with a family. She tells her own daughter what it was like to live in a paradise on the Adriatic Sea where resources like electricity and water had to be used with prudence. She tells them her family had a hard time making ends meet like everyone else in their town, and they should be grateful for the opportunities they have in their new home.

Then I look at the next person who walks by and see another future unfold. So many lives wandering about, oblivious to their insignificance, yet full of meaning. My travels have made me aware of this strange paradox. I am all too aware of my own insignificance. And yet, my smallness does not bother me. It has made me realize that I do not need to be so afraid of talking to people – they are often willing to help, and anyways, the encounter is often forgotten a moment later.

It is four in the morning when I nervously walk the empty streets and ascend the cobblestone steps. I exit the great stone walls of Dubrovnik to take a cab to the airport. I feel resolved to continue to explore this curious world and its strange contents. In travel, I am a quiet observer of the marks left by history; a silent witness to the workings of the daily mundane; an attentive audience to the many stories within people. Rather than let fear of the unknown hinder me, I will let the search for the unknown guide me. And there is so much more to explore.

Dubrovnik at 4:00 a.m.

Jennifer Armstrong

Jennifer Armstrong is from Toronto, Canada. She works as a teacher of music, visual art, and English. She enjoys drawing and painting, composing and performing music, reading, writing, archaeology, teaching both at home and abroad, and exploring the world. She has been to over 60 countries as of 2018 and hopes to visit all countries within the next decade.

Instagram: https://www.instagram.com/vespertravels

To All the Warriors I May One Day Meet

by Sarah Haringcaspel

TRAVELLING! We should all do it at one point, or another. I've had several great opportunities in my life that allowed me to start travelling when I was as young as 13 years old. You see, I used to be a bit of a choir geek - choir captain in both primary school and high school as well as being in another public choir in my spare time for 16 years. So, when I was in grade 12, I was in three different choirs and by graduation I had been on three different tours through Europe and another to South Korea.

I am under no delusions. I am extremely lucky to have had even the chance *presented* to me to go on any or all of these trips, let alone ACTUALLY going on them. My family is by no means wealthy, but my parents' minds were set on us attending private schools for our high school education (made possible thanks to half-scholarships) and I am extremely grateful for the opportunities that I had growing up and for the support of not only my family but those that made these opportunities realities.

When it comes to my inspiration for travelling, I can say with complete certainty that my first overseas choir tour to South Korea was the dream-defining trip, which set me on my current course. We were one of many choirs that were to take part in the 'World Vision Children's Choir Festival' in Seoul. As part of the trip, our choir was hosted by the World Vision Korean Children's Choir and their families. My friend and I were billeted with a couple and their three children, the eldest of which I became very close with. I remember on our first night in Korea, I couldn't sleep because of the anxiety that comes with going to a new country for the first time and living with strangers. I stayed awake for the majority of the night, and all the while, I remember seeing my host mum in the kitchen with dozens of dishes brewing and bubbling away into the wee hours of the morning. When it finally came for everyone to wake up, I swear, she was still there, cooking and preparing the scrumptious meal we were about to receive. We packed away the floor bedding on which we slept, and in the same room, we pulled out two low tables, one for the dad and one for the rest of us. This is when the mother begins laying down all of her efforts, Bulgogi, soup, an entire fish that had been cooked in something that made it bright red, and so much more. The meal covered the entire table! And this was breakfast!! I was absolutely taken aback by how much food there was, and it was to die for.

During our stay, my friend and I were selected to be followed around by a local T.V. station's camera crew, which meant that wherever we went, we were privately escorted around by a manager of whatever venue we were going to. One particular memory that stands out in my mind was when our host family took us to 'Lotte World' (a big indoor theme park in Seoul). We were greeted by the manager or somebody important in Lotte World, who escorted us around the park. He got us to the front of lines, treated us to lunch, and gave us flowers... (all in front of the cameras of course), but WOW, it was one hell of a day. Again, no delusions, I am so so so lucky for being able to have that experience.

I have many other amazing memories of this trip including visiting the night markets with my host dad and of course the choir festival itself, in which I got to meet people from all over the world and see all their different styles of music and performance.

As the final day in Korea came, I was changed. I had come to Korea not knowing what to expect, and rather afraid, but I left knowing that Korea was a relatively safe, welcoming place with amazing people, food and culture. I was young, but I knew I would be back; somehow, I was going to find a way to be there again.

Skip ahead 12 years and one bachelor's degree later, and here I am, living and working in South Korea, it's like a damn fairy-tale.

And So it Begins...

As I mentioned before, during high school, I had three more tour opportunities, two with my school's elite show-choir (we danced, had shiny costumes and everything!) and another with the same choir that took me to Korea, 'The Brisbane Birralee Voices'. All of which were unique and valuable experiences and opportunities that I will cherish forever, but without doubt, my first trip to South Korea is what lit the fire under my ass.

When it comes to travelling, there are always going to be doubts in your mind, either put there by your parents, by the media or by whatever. My first four international trips were all tours with large groups, and so, I was able to experience the excitement and wonder of travelling in a safe and structured environment. This had a lot of benefits, the greatest of which was to take away my fear of leaving home, leaving what was comfortable and familiar, but perhaps it made me a little too brazen. Which leads me to CHINA...

One day, I was sitting at home on my computer, job searching on a site called 'Gumtree'. It was here that I came across the ad for an "internship" teaching English in China. To be fair, I was not in the healthiest head space at university for a variety of reasons. So, at this point I thought "Screw it! Let's go to China for six months!" I really don't think I considered it for too long. I already had a friend who had deferred his course at university for a year, so I knew that it was possible. Anyway, I emailed my university admin to double check the details and logistics of taking a six-month sabbatical. Once it was clear that there was nothing holding me back, I applied to the agency in China (through Gumtree) and within the space of about two months, my flights were booked, I had my visa, and I was trying to comfort my dear confused mother... bless her.

I feel like I should probably give a little bit more background... If any of you know the site Gumtree, it's basically just a free ad service, similar to craigslist. I had gotten several great jobs through this site in the past and even found my beautiful fluff-ball of a cat on there! But in retrospect, I probably should've been a bit more cautious applying to a random-ass company <u>IN CHINA</u>. Obviously, I'm here to tell the tale so it wasn't a complete disaster... in fact, I prefer to refer to it as 'The Great Learning Experience' *through gritted teeth* but as you may have caught on, there were one or two moments of ... *pause for effect* ... unease.

The Great Wall of China, Badaling section

The Great Learning Experience

The Great Learning Experience, much like the Great Wall of China; steep, treacherous and lacking in emergency exits or amenities. At the end, it left my legs shaking, my eyes watering slightly, a sense of relief and of course, lessons learned. I'm definitely a more 'act first, ask questions later' sort of person, especially when it comes to travelling. Perhaps by writing about my experiences here, more level-headed people will be able to learn from my mistakes.

Before I start, I just want to say that I LOVED travelling in China and I would absolutely do it again. The following account specifically has to do with the company I was hired by to teach and the visa that they advised me to get.

As I said, I was in China for six months at the beginning of 2015; arriving in mid-January and departing in mid-July. The first three months were as you would expect for your first solo travel/work experience, I was a little homesick, I was excited, and I was busy working and trying to see as much as I could in my spare time. Where was I, you ask? Beijing. Anyone who has ever been there will tell you it's an enormous, sprawling city with some of the most fascinating and breathtaking historical sites I have ever seen. Something I always say about Beijing, is that you could live there for years and never see everything there is to see. There is always something more just around the corner, be it food, history, niche stores or cafes as well as art and theatre, Beijing has it all!

When in Beijing, I was also living with a family, just as I was in Korea, so I especially loved experiencing China from a local's perspective.

My job was advertised as an "English teaching internship in a local Kindergarten," however, after arriving, it quickly became apparent that I was the main teacher and I had one local teaching assistant in a fairly small and VERY new school (they were still putting in the flooring when I arrived). I would work every day from Monday to Friday, as well as every second Saturday. On top of my school duties, I was spending most of my spare time with the host family and their children (specifically their eldest 4-year-old son). I don't want to toot my own horn too much but after just a month, this boy-who was getting most of my attention (and all of my love)-went from speaking NO English, to being able to have decent conversations (for an above-average four-year-old).

Skip three months ahead, it's just your usual Wednesday; I get a call from a mate in the same program as me (with the same company). He tells me that he just got out of a seven-day stint in prison and that I should stop working immediately. I hang up the phone and instantly burst into tears, mostly from shock, but you could also say fear had something to do with it. Once I gained some composure, I called my host mother and boss (she owned the kindergarten in which I was working) and she tells me not to worry. She assured me that she had friends in the police-force and nothing was going to happen to me, that my safety was the most important thing, and that she would not make me work at the kindergarten anymore. After discussing the issue with her over the next few days, we both decided that I should break away from the company that brought me to China and instead au pair for the family and take care of her son exclusively. I didn't want to go home yet, I was really enjoying my life in China (you know, aside from the possibility of arrest, deportation and a permanent black spot on my record), so this really was the best I could hope for (I also couldn't really afford to go home at this point). I really was the luckiest person, to have had this amazing family, and this astounding woman on my side.

The issue was my visa; I had come to China for an 'internship' and I trusted that the company was doing everything above board. Unfortunately, the company left a bit to be desired, either by active choice or by accident, I don't know. My company had told me that because it was an 'internship,' I should apply for a student visa and not a working visa. This was wrong. Our contract conditions in China in fact made us eligible for working visas and *ineligible* for student visas. I should also note, that the only reason my mate was let out of jail and not deported was because he was married to a Chinese-national, if this hadn't been the case, he would probably have been kept in jail until forcibly removed from the country.

The company also had an au pair program and I knew after listening to my fair share of gossip and a decent amount of research, that you CAN au pair in China with a student visa, so I knew that our solution was an option.

Now, I didn't just suddenly decide to distrust the company and put all of my faith in my host mother. Over the previous three months, there had been several people in my company who had experienced issues with their contracts, or employers or whatever else, in some cases leading to them having to leave the country. THIS is the reason I distrusted them, and I didn't want to associate with them in the event that the police would track my friend who was detained and follow the paper trail to me. After I made my decision to leave the company, they kept contacting me, asking what my plans were. Because of some of the fine print in my contract, they had to "officially see me off." So, I lied. I told them that I was quitting my job, leaving the family and that I had booked a flight for the day after next. They said that they would pay for my accommodation for two nights and I felt it would have looked suspicious if I had refused. So I fake-packed my big suitcase, got in a car they sent for me and I spent two nights in a hostel on the other side of the city. Now that I was officially off their radar, I got on the subway and made my way back to my Chinese family. It was all a bit co-op really.

    I think what was most scary about this situation was that I had little-to-no contact with the outside world. As you may or may not know, China has a pretty intense block on internet usage, meaning, no Facebook, no Google, no Gmail. Of course, I had a VPN when I was over there, but it was very unreliable and I couldn't use it for more than 15-20 minutes at a time. Because I wasn't able to really contact anyone for emotional support, I had to deal with everything on my own for the most part, and that was pretty hard. But I came out the other side having learned my lesson; do your damn research about the company you are going with and the visa that you need, don't just trust them to tell you what you should have, and mayyyybeee don't look on Gumtree for this sort of job.

I'm sure that many people here could've seen this coming; keep in mind that I was pretty young and naive when this happened and China is notorious for having a pretty complicated visa system.

The Reasons You SHOULD Go to China (Besides the Great Wall and Beijing)

Taken at the local park near where I lived.

Now let's talk about what came next; what I loved about China and the places you should visit.

I was in China for six months in total, as I said before, I was teaching in a kindergarten for the first three months and then I was an au pair for two months. At this point the family I was living with decided to go back to their hometown to see their relatives for three weeks, which meant that I would be spending my last few weeks in China hanging out in Beijing mostly alone (as my other friends were working during the week), which

I was TOTALLY fine with. But, lucky for me, my host mother had other plans. She decided to give me a bonus (not part of my original contract) to thank me for teaching her son and I guess just because she loved me so much *hair flick* ...you know. She told me to take the money and "go see more of China," because it's an immense, beautiful and pretty diverse country.

I already had been putting away half of my salary each month, plus the bonus, and it was more than enough for me to travel around for a few weeks, so I set to planning. I grabbed a map and pin-pointed all of the places that were on the top of my list, checked out the train lines between each place and made a loop back up to Beijing.

Technically, this was my first time travelling for an extended period of time as more of a backpacker AND on my own. Despite (or perhaps, to spite) the past, I didn't really think about the things that could go wrong, except for possible scheduling issues. During my time in the school, I had also become very close with my co-teacher who was Chinese-Mongolian and when I told her I was planning a trip, she suggested kicking it off with a trip together to the city of Hohhot in Inner Mongolia (an autonomous region of China - not to be confused with Mongolia the independent country) which was near her home-town.

Hohhot City Mosque, Inner Mongolia

It was a seven-hour train trip from Beijing to Hohhot, we arrived in the late afternoon and had dinner at a local lamb barbeque place (because you MUST have lamb in Mongolia) where we sat on the street, eating delicious lamb skewers covered in chili flakes and cumin, drinking a local beer with some of her mates from university. After dinner, my friend decided to go to bed, while I went for an evening stroll around the hotel and to maybe find some more lamb. I came across a beautiful Mosque that was lit up via a coloured light display and in front had an enormous Genie lamp, after my wandering, and upsetting lack of lamb, I decided to go back to the hotel. The next morning, I heard prayers being played over loudspeakers in the city and I thought back to the wonderful mosque that I had witnessed the evening before, and pondered the essence of religion, life and death ... the usual.

The next day, we got picked up early by another friend and he drove us a few hours out of the city and into the grasslands of Inner Mongolia, I can't say exactly where we were, but damn, it gave life back into the phrase 'wide open spaces'. I literally could not see anything other than the dirt road on which we were driving, grass and uninterrupted blue skies. We made it to a hotel-style "Yurt camp" (a yurt is a traditional Mongolian tent); I say hotel-style, because the entire camp had about thirty very large, permanent, yurts on concrete foundations with an attached toilet and electricity. I personally felt that the lack of authenticity in the living quarters took away slightly from the experience, but that was soon forgotten with the help of horses, a bonfire, a feast, and yes, alcohol. Horse riding on Mongolian horses was definitely the highlight of this trip, and I would absolutely recommend others to go horse riding in the grasslands.

After we got back to Hohhot, we stayed another night, which meant more drinks and more food, and the next day I headed to Xi-an.

Xi-an, Shaanxi Province

You may have heard of Xi-an, the city known for housing the Terracotta Warriors (I later found out that the warriors are, in fact housed two hours outside of town). The terracotta warriors were awe-inspiring... as much as you would expect for something that old and that grand. You might think I don't sound super enthusiastic about them, but to be fair, I had just had a 15-hour train ride from Hohhot the day before and then had to make the four-hour round trip to the massive museum where they were housed. I think, my favourite part of Xi-an was actually the area around my hostel. It was located in the 'Muslim quarter' and I found the sights, sounds and smells highly stimulating, plus the people were so friendly.

The Grasslands of Inner Mongolia

Chengdu, Sichuan province

After Xi-an, I made my way to Chengdu, which had been described to me by everyone I told, as the 'lazy city' of China (the local opinion) and I was like "HELL YEAH!" after spending the last 5 months in Beijing... I was ready to get me some LAZY! and really, it was just like my hometown to be honest, which, I guess has some deeper implications about Chinese culture and my own temperament. Honestly, if I was to ever go back and live in China, I would go to Chengdu, it WAS a city but it also had some amazing natural scenery surrounding it as well as a more laid-back atmosphere, ESPECIALLY compared to Beijing.

For reference, if you've ever seen those videos of people playing with a bunch of baby pandas, it was probably in Chengdu, because that is where the WWF Panda sanctuary is, and the original draw-card for my visit. Unfortunately, I didn't get to play with the baby pandas (it just didn't work out), but upon more research of the area, I found out about something called DaFu (Big Buddha), which, as the name suggests was a big-ass buddha statue painstakingly hand-carved out of the side of a cliff over the course of 100 years. The buddha is overlooking the rocks and waves below and is a symbol of safe travel for ship-merchants going through the area. This statue was HUGE, and beautiful and it was surrounded by nature on all sides, as well as several temples. I absolutely loved this place and it is my second recommendation, if you ever get the chance.

Da Fu (Big Buddha), Chengdu.

Here's a brief amusing anecdote while I was in the vicinity of DaFu: After climbing up, down, and around this statue, I decided to go on a little adventure in the opposite direction of the many other tourists. This adventure lasted all of 10 minutes-I was walking down a forested path, minding my own business, when suddenly I heard a rustle in the trees above and slightly in front of where I was walking. I take a few steps back, just as two snakes (150cm long each) fall from the low canopy to about three meters in front of me - quick math; together, they were the same length as the distance between myself and them-thankfully, luck stuck again that day, in that the two had fallen from the tree because they were either fighting between themselves or rather aggressively trying to make little snake babies, and therefore were too distracted to notice little old me. After they "struggled" out of sight, I decided that I'd had enough of that adventure and chose to take the road more travelled... nature's a wonderful thing, don't you agree? *Amusing anecdote over.*

Chengdu had other fascinating things to see including temples and face-changing theatre. I also met some people that were going to climb a nearby mountain range (specifically, Emei Peak) on which, you can apparently break through the cloud line and see the clouds as more of an ocean. I say 'apparently' because I did not have enough time to make the climb up and down the mountain and still fit in the other cities on my list. This just gives me another good reason to visit again.

Yangshuo, Guilin Province

After Chengdu was Yangshuo, a small but fairly touristy town sitting along the famous 'Li River.' In Yangshuo, I got on a "boat" made of plumbers tubing as well as witnessing the AMAZING light and water show called the "Impression of Sanjie Liu" (curated by the same guy who put together the 2008 Olympic Ceremony, Zhang Yimou)-although this was a huge tourist attraction, it was DEFINITELY worth it. For me though, my favourite part of Yangshuo was meeting the other travellers, two of whom were a couple from Romania who invited me to join them on a hire-bike adventure to see the 'Big Banyan Tree' and 'moon hill.' The ride itself was breathtaking (in more ways than one) and the couple were fantastic people who made the adventure even more delightful.

Yangshuo also saw me meet three gentlemen with whom I got along famously. One was a very nice dutchman and the other two, funnily enough, had their birthdays on either side of mine in the same month (4th, 5th, 6th) ... we saw this as something like FATE and decided to get wildly drunk and explore the streets of Yangshuo at 3 in the morning. It was a fantastic night of jocularity and friendship, and I still receive postcards from one of them, three years later. Honestly, meeting people whilst travelling should be a priority if you want to really enjoy your time there, the people you meet will usually be experiencing it for the first time as well, so you will have so much to talk about. As for the people who are locals, they know the area and can show you some hidden gems, so you should befriend them too! I have also found that other travellers are some of the most open-minded, caring and friendly people out there, I have never felt unsafe around those that I've met while travelling.

Li River, Guilin Province.

Lastly, Shanghai

How should I describe Shanghai… I'm going to go with WET. Almost as soon as I arrived at my hostel in Shanghai, it began to rain and it didn't stop until I got back to Beijing four days later. I didn't let this dampen my spirits, I actually quite love the rain. Instead, I made it my mission to eat as many dumplings as I could, and I believe I succeeded. Now, whenever it rains, I have an insatiable craving for dumplings. I also visited a few gardens and temples in Shanghai; I'm not much for shopping, so I didn't see the point in braving the weather for a new pair of sunglasses. I did however, meet many people in my hostel (because most people just stayed inside next to the in-house bar) and one night, our company of about 10 people, decided to try and go to a club that supposedly had a live shark. Unfortunately, the men in our posse were underdressed (it was a very fancy shark, you see) and we did not make it in. We did still find a cool bar to hang out in and I had myself a romantic (non-sexual) interlude in the rain with one member of our group, so that definitely was an upside to the rain (without it, I daresay it would've been much less romantic). The next day was full of more dumplings, forbidden love and more rain.

DUMPLINGS EVERY DAY! Treat yo' self.

Coming to an End

At the beginning of my trip, before I had even left my home country, I actually booked my return flights home for July. Because of another slight, visa-based issue, I had to leave China a week earlier than my booked flights (which I fixed quite simply and at very little extra expense.) I had booked a set of flights to get back to my home country with a layover in Seoul. Beijing to Seoul is a very short flight, so I simply changed the first flight to Seoul to be a week earlier and left the original flight from Seoul to home the same. During my extra week in South Korea, I also decided to fly down to Jeju Island for a few days (for my birthday) and ended up really loving the experience. I was pretty pleased with myself for successfully avoiding a big cancellation fee and making the most of that time in Korea. However, I would not pre-book flights again. I think in that situation, it would be better to wait until I know the exact dates of my visa.

Camelia Hill on Jeju Island, South Korea

After the great learning experience, I managed to make it to July with my sanity mostly intact but as I said before, I was a bit shook after my experience in China. However, I do not regret going to China and I will absolutely go back at some point to travel or to work. Although some of the experiences were tough at the time, I think that I was lucky enough and safe enough, that I wasn't put-off by China. In the end, I was sad to be leaving, I had my Chinese family, I had the little boy that I was taking care of 24/7, I had friends ... and THE FOOD, oh man, the food! (which is NOTHING like western-style Chinese food - I had ZERO spring rolls, fried rice or sweet and sour pork while living there.)

All in all, I think the good experiences outweighed the bad, and I learned many things while on this adventure that I think are valuable for my future in travel and in life (Let's be honest, I'm one of those "optimists" people always talk about.)

~~~

There is something that I haven't mentioned yet... and that is my identity, and I think I owe it to myself and my community to talk about my experiences as a queer person in the countries that I have travelled to as best as I can. I identify as queer (or fluid) and non-binary, with she/her pronouns. This just means that I live my life however I want or feel on a day-to-day, month-to-month, or year-to-year basis and I do not live by the influence of binary expectations from society. I have only recently come to this knowledge (as it currently stands), and as a queer person, I am also accepting of change as time goes on and as I change both physically and mentally.

Over the last few years (including my time in China) I have seen many changes, when I was in China, for instance, I identified as a lesbian and I had never had experiences with men (that romantic interlude/forbidden romance in Shanghai ring any bells?). As it was my first time overseas, alone, as an out queer person, I had done some prior research into the laws in China concerning the LGBTQI+ community. The laws stating that homosexuality was a mental illness had only been overturned in 2001 and it seemed like there was little to no protection against discrimination. I decided that it was safer for me to keep my sexual-identity private. Unfortunately, at the time that I left for China, I was dating a woman (let's call her Polly) and between the lack of internet access and privacy, it quickly fizzled out. Before we broke up, my host-mother would ask me if I had a boyfriend and I would simply say yes but never referred to Polly as a boy or 'my boyfriend' myself, I simply referred to Polly as 'my partner' or 'them/they.' This technique is pretty common, I think, for avoiding confrontation, and was the same technique I used when I was in the closet and unfortunately, I do still currently employ this method in South Korea, particularly within my workplace. Just before I left for my adventure around China, my host mother asked me directly, "Do you love women" and I said "yes." This does give me hope and I know that there are many people who will accept and not discriminate, but it's the not knowing that makes it difficult and causes anxiety for many people.

    I used to think that I could live with hiding who I am in specific parts of my life, but honestly, it does become exhausting, and those times when I slip-up can cause quite a bit of anxiety. This is one of the reasons why I no longer see myself staying in South Korea much further into the future. This does not mean that Korea doesn't have a thriving queer community or that I am surrounded by hate, but personally, I don't want to live in fear that my employers will find out that I'm queer and I will lose my job because if it (which is a possibility as South Korea lacks any LGBTQI+ anti-discrimination laws and still has work to do in term of gender equality- for locals as well.) I know that this fear is within me and there are still many places where my situation would be the same or much worse, and of course, my situation doesn't compare at all to what some people are going through in their lives. I am just thinking about my own future and what I want it to look like.

Camelia Hill, Jeju. Symbol of Jeju

There are still certain places where I know that I would not feel safe because of my gender and sexual identity. I do not want to make accusations about any specific country, but there are still many places in the world where homosexuality is illegal and several that still recognise the death penalty. Personally, I would not travel to these places right now, because I am truly frightened of what could happen even if I am merely *suspected* of being gay (even without proof.) There are also several countries that have neutral laws concerning LGBTQI+ peoples, but in some cases, the public takes punishment into their own hands, with no investigation, protections or repercussions.

Here is Where I Will Leave You

This being said, I have learned a lot from travelling and the people I've met. The biggest influence from travelling has been that no matter how old you are or whatever decisions you've made and wherever you are right now, that does not define your future. YOU have the power to do whatever you want in life and go wherever you want to go. Try not to let fear or uncertainty control your actions, YOU ARE A POWERFUL, DRIVEN, UNIQUE INDIVIDUAL AND YOU ARE CAPABLE OF ANYTHING. *I try to keep this on repeat in my head, and something that I still work on every day.*

I was always self-conscious about several things (as many people are,) but my body-weight in particular. At some point in my life I became under the impression that because I was overweight, this would stop me from doing certain things. But travelling and living in different countries has put me in situations where I had no choice but to do the things I was nervous about and forced me to come to the realization that I can do whatever I have to do, whatever I WANT to do, and whatever I set my mind to. The other people I have met have also been a massive positive influence for me, even if I have only known them for an hour, we encourage each other to be brave and do what we want to do.

I think it's important to have goals, and one of mine is to become more of an activist for my community and to network and perhaps use travelling as a way to understand and help people be free and embrace their true identities. I still have a long way to go in terms of overcoming my fears and making this goal a reality, but like I said, I have all the time in the world. I can figure it out at my own pace and I can make my mark, in my own way.

I am currently following that dream that came to be when I was just a wee lass of 13, living and working in South Korea. But this is not where my story ends … My feet are starting to itch. It's almost time for a new chapter.

To be continued...

Sarah Haringcaspel

Now, you might be wondering where I'm from, I'll give you some hints ... let's see how you go...

1. Our country was invaded by the British .... Too broad?
2. We are the only continent without an active volcano.
3. Our country is currently made up of 6 states and 2 territories.
4. This is the official flag of one of the native populations.

5. Our country is home to the largest cattle station in the world.
6. Our country is home to six of the top ten deadliest snakes in the world. (Getting close?)
7. Although our country is commonly associated with warm weather, one region snows more than the Swiss Alps!
8. We have a small population in comparison to the very large mass of land on which we live.

9. We say words such as "bonza" which means "great," "fair dinkum" which can be used as a question and an affirmation (i.e. "Seriously?" "Seriously." / "fair dinkum?" "Fair dinkum.") and "Whoop Whoop" which can be used as the name of any place in the middle of nowhere.
10. And last but not least, as of 2017 we officially have marriage equality!

I'm sure you know the answer by now and perhaps you even learned a little bit about the Great Down Under.

I grew up in the suburbs of Brisbane in Queensland, Australia. I left Australia after I graduated from university to pursue my love of travel and to live and work in foreign countries. I currently live near Busan, South Korea and am working as an English teacher in the EPIK (Public school) program here. I love children, as well as singing and performance which is most likely the reason, I love teaching so much, because I get to be surrounded by children every day, to entertain and help them reach their goals. I really love this life that I was given and the path that I have chosen, It is exciting not knowing where I may be in 5 years' time. Germany? Taiwan? Spain? Who knows!? BRING IT ON.

PS. Respect people's identities and pronouns.

The Truths and Dares of Travel

by Akanksha Holani

I was the first girl of my generation, born in a family that had always wanted a daughter more than a son; but the testosterone in our genes runs strong! However, on a rainy monsoon night in the tropical forests of northeast India, my family got their girl – their desire; or as I would be called 22 years later – the Hindi synonym of desire, *Akanksha*.

Well, the good thing was my family didn't quite know how to raise a girl differently from a boy! They thought that all children must be raised alike. So, I grew up playing with action figures and had a boyish haircut; poking the eyes out of my Barbies whenever I came across one, because I didn't know what to do with a plastic doll!

However, my favorite thing to do was listen to my Dada (Grandfather) tell me about the time he went to Uttrakhand and conquered the Himalayas; and the time he went to the extreme south of India and rested on the beaches. He had so many tales to tell! While other kids just wanted to hear stories of *Panchtantra*, his stories found a fan in the only girl of the family.

I decided I must someday live these stories too. I was never told that I couldn't ... until the world changed in December 2012! "A young woman gangraped in Delhi" was the worst news we had ever woken up to! Innocent women, walking from their offices to their homes, were not safe. Women of 25 years of age, then 20, then, 15...then 8, 4, even 2 months? Brutally raped and thrown off to die!

What had suddenly gone so wrong? Was it always this way? I couldn't contemplate how my family had dared to raise a single girl in a world where women were no longer being treated as humans. Women never really were humans in our society; as far as history dates, India worshiped women as goddesses; and now women were dolls with poked out eyes and tattered clothes?!

My family realized that this world did not raise boys and girls the same, but they did what they could to protect their girl. I had planned to move to Delhi to further my studies, but they told me I couldn't go there.

I didn't blame them for it. I found a safer city, Mumbai, to continue my studies.

In a way, Mumbai made me. Something changes in you the day you decide to earn your living. Oftentimes people confuse freedom with independence. You always have the freedom to do what you want; however, can you do it on your own? That's independence! Attaining financial independence at 20 gave me the confidence to survive on my own.

I lived for four years alone in one of the world's most expensive cities.

However, this wasn't the dream, at least not mine. A nine to five job in Mumbai wasn't where I intended to stay. I had to live my stories. But now, I was being told that I couldn't! I would fly every month to my home, Jaipur; because that's how homesick I would get. Dinners started getting bitter with discussions over why I couldn't travel, until one night, over dessert, my mother told me, "If you want to, just go."

"But you know how unsafe the world is out there?" I sounded a lot like my protective father.

"You haven't seen it yet!" was one of those answers where she wouldn't say much but would tell a lot.

"What if something happens to me?"

"If you think so, it will. Go out with hopes, not fears. Your grandfather is an old man in his 60s, nobody robs him or harms him. He still travels; he would want you to travel."

This conversation stayed with me forever. I took the leap; and decided to go to Sikkim, a northeastern state of India, famous for the Himalayas and its Buddhist-Indian culture. That's where it all began.

The Journey so Far...

It's been 2 years now, and here I stand with 12 countries ticked off on my list, all alone – and full of happy memories! Well, some wounds too…like the wound on my knee that I got in Belgium!

I started out with a commentator's view on India, that it isn't safe; especially cities like Delhi and Noida. In two years, I have been there on countless occasions. I have travelled to the remotest parts of India, because that's where the tourists don't go, and you can swim in the bluest waterfalls hiding in plain sight. I have travelled to the Indian desert in Rajasthan and Gujarat. I have also been to the extreme north-eastern states that are yet to be plagued by tourists; the states where nature meets history! I have travelled to the Indian tribal islands too, where apparently "Oh, the tribals are not welcoming, they kill mainlanders!" but here is the news, I received nothing but warmth from the locals.

A Secret Waterfall in North-East India

The minute you tell someone you are travelling alone, their instincts would be to care for you; not harm you! "Oh, you are travelling alone. Here, take this knife with you;" a Kashmiri tribal woman handed me the only knife she kept for her defense.

India is a huge country, the seventh largest to be exact. India should ideally be a continent, because our states are more like separate countries. We do have similarities, but more differences – different languages, different beliefs, different ethnicities etc.; but all these mini-countries have still agreed upon being together as one country. As cute as that is, it is still a huge country where most travelers get confused. I had perceptions about all the other states, and as I crossed them one after another, I realized I was wrong about every state. This got me planning to go beyond my homeland. I had perceptions about other countries, too.

To Travel is to Know, Not Assume...

I had heard things. I had my own prejudices. Here's the thing about prejudices – they only exist where there is no experience. Once you have the experience, then you have facts.

"In Paris, people don't help you if you don't speak in French." When you travel, you realize you were wrong about every place.

"Scandinavians are cold," "Germans are boring and serious," and "Switzerland has the world's most beautiful mountains." To be true, I always knew this one, in particular, was over-exaggerated. I mean, I come from a country that has the longest chain of Himalayas. I was pretty sure that when I get to visit Switzerland, I wouldn't be quite impressed. And as expected, The Alps failed in front of The Himalayas, but Switzerland didn't fail to impress me. Happiness was found in tender fondues, sweet locals, and train journeys across Interlaken. I was correct about the Himalayas being beautiful, but a flight across the Arctic Circle shattered my old beliefs of them being the "absolute" beauty!

Travelling makes you realize that there are no "absolutes" or "best." If you travel right, you would never be able to answer – Which country or city did you like the most?

Every time I come back from a trip, I ponder on the places I went and what I experienced. However, the people around me look at it like a competition or like a battle for the "best place I visited." The truth is – Alps, Himalayas, Arctic; now that I look back at them, there was no comparison. Alps didn't lose. Arctic didn't win. Are they all alike? Possibly, structurally! Are they all different? Entirely! Which one is better? That's just irrelevant.

We go out looking for full-stops to our question marks, but travel instead gives you peaceful silences, that would take paragraphs if you tried describing that emotion.

They say a memory is never exact. It is the recreation of past by our brains; so science says every time you recall something, you are recreating that experience.

Every time you recall your journey, you are recreating it with the lessons you didn't quite understand back then, with the emotions you couldn't quite express – and that is why every time you think of it again and again, you travel all over again. The more you look back at it, the more you pick up on the details you hadn't noticed earlier.

Travel doesn't leave you with a return ticket. It doesn't stop when you conclude your vacation and come back home. You might think so, that the chapter is over now, but it is not. Every time you hear that place's name; you will turn back and pick up straight from where you left off. Travel never leaves you. What might get reduced to some photos or souvenirs is actually a part of your existence.

Once you have been to a place, a part of you becomes a part of it. That place leaves pieces in your life. So, today I like my coffee Finnish and my french fries better be Dutch. I, to this day, wonder why I love the Eiffel Tower the way I do!

Travel makes you question yourself. You might think you know yourself, but the farther you go, the less you plan; you'll be amazed to know that you were wrong about most parts!

For someone who dwells in the mountains and jumps in waterfalls, why was the best part about Switzerland Zurich? For someone who only goes where nobody does, why do I want to go back to Paris? And no matter where I go, why do my taste buds get more and more sure that nothing comes close to Indian food?

Why does my imaginary happy place have the tulips of Netherlands combined with the Aurora Borealis of Norway? It is a little bit of everything that I have experienced.

Aurora Borealis in the middle of the Atlantic Ocean

My happy place has 15 countries without their borders. Travel has made me realize the concept of borders is stupid. If people could just travel more and further than they think they can, this world would be a happier place. Travel breaks it down to you that landscapes, people, cultures – aren't all that different; but a whole new world entirely, every time you find a new one.

Take me for an example. I am a hardcore vegetarian. You aren't racist for thinking that all Indians live off vegetables and curries. We do love our curries!

However, this will be another one of those misconceived myths you have about India; because most Indians aren't vegetarian in reality. But I am!

For a Vegetarian like me, Scandinavia should have been unappetizing with all their *lutafisk* and *Brennivin* shots. But I loved it. When I started traveling, I couldn't sit in a non-vegetarian place. The idea of animals being butchered in the very same kitchen would make me sick.

However, the more I travelled the more I realized there are so many perspectives. In many Asian cultures, animal sacrifice is a way of life. They base their practices on the belief that their deities will be pleased with the offerings. Travel opened me up to believing that some people will have views very different from yours, so much so that you wouldn't want to waste a second before you yell at them–"You are wrong." Travel opened me up to letting different belief systems co-exist. You don't necessarily have to revamp your belief system, they don't either. You could try and understand why different people do what they do "Why do Icelanders have a drink made out of whale's liver?"

But even if you don't understand it entirely, travel opens you up to respecting them nonetheless. Travel, in fact, opened me up so much that I went ahead and tried that *God Damn* drink, the *Brennivin* shots! They were horrible, but no regrets!

The Black Sand Beach of Iceland During a Storm

Stories that Change You!

Humanity stands enforced again, every time someone truly travels. It is when you get lost in a foreign country, where no one speaks your language; that you realize how important your own language is. Something you have taken for granted-your culture, your people, perhaps, even your country!

While travelling across one of the Belgian villages, I got my ATM card blocked. Was I stupid enough to travel with a single card? Definitely!

But to think that organizing your money or planning your expenses is the answer, that is more stupid! My money laid there in my card, all loaded but of no use. Not to forget that I was on my period and had to limp my way across that silent town on a rainy day. Limping because I had been partying too much in Prague two days back and you know how that goes...

It seemed horrible. Just two days ago, I was partying in some of the best clubs of Europe. How fate changes! I was so proud that I had earned this trip, so proud that I got that *moolah;* but this trip had a lesson planned for me.

Fast forward to Belgium. Now I am broke and broken! I sat down on the grass crying, wondering if I should call my parents. I should have, but you know when you are the only child, you are more worried about breaking your parents' hearts than your own. "They had always warned me about this, hadn't they? I had travelled enough to be more cautious than this, hadn't I?" But this was all no use, was it?

An old Belgian woman saw me there. She came to me. You would think that all white people assume all brown people are terrorists; at least that's how the media thinks! She didn't.

She asked me a question in Dutch and I replied in English. I understood she wasn't getting a word I said. I started waving my ATM card and then, my bills and my passport. Everything in my purse was out on the grass, in an attempt to make her understand that I was scared.

She picked them all one-by-one and put them back, then got up with my purse. I had heard about the French being thieves and that you had to be careful with your luggage when in Paris; but in Ghent too!?

She was an old woman, I would say, in her 60s. She then said in a heavy Dutch accent, "Come, home!" No, this punctuation isn't an error. She said in a way as if she was calling me "home."

She got me to her place, made some warm waffles and all the while, said nothing. Was I a fool for trusting a complete stranger? Perhaps she had mixed something in those waffles. That explains why despite only having waffles on my 4-day trip across Belgium, hers were the best! No, it wasn't the fact that it was raining or that her room had that welcoming fragrance; but the fact that I felt okay, I felt "home."

A lot of people would think it was just luck. Again, a lot of people would think that you need money to travel. But there I was – with money but of no use! That day wasn't about the places I had seen or the rain or the card going all crazy, it was about that old lady.

You can go years and years, building your walls, believing that everyone out there just wants to hurt you; and then one stranger can shatter it all. She even dropped me to the nearest bank the next day, I got my card fixed and she patiently waited with me the whole time. She didn't strike me as a woman who had so much free time on hand, but I think she stayed to make sure I was not scared again. Every once in a while, when our eyes would meet - she would randomly smile. I took her to get a coffee, I figured that was the least I could do since she just wouldn't accept any cash. She left on her pink bicycle, probably back to home or on another rescue mission. My superwoman came on a bicycle!

If You Don't Believe in Magic, Travel More Often!

Travel makes you believe in magic, makes you want to question – why is maturity related with bitterness? Why do we even have trust issues?

In Norway, I was looking for the Aurora Borealis. At two in the morning. In -12 degrees Celsius, all alone. Lost in the middle of nowhere on one of the remotest islands of Arctic Circle! Well, they did tell me that the hunt for Northern lights isn't an easy one.

There were a few homes there. I banged on each of those doors, hoping someone would open it up and let me in; but perhaps, people don't like staying up till 2 AM in chilly temperatures! I was on my own, or so I thought.

A drunken Norwegian man's figure started coming out of the snow-caked pine trees and as he came closer, I regretted not having brought along my knife. Yes, the same one the Kashmiri woman gave me. Of course, I keep some things close to me!

Anyway, he was at a distance of some two feet, I didn't even make an attempt to look at him; the island was in the middle of a blizzard. I was barely even managing to stand straight, let alone try to see the other person's face.

He asks me in a very drunken way, "Are you lost too?"

"Yes, I am not used to this much cold. Can you please tell me where is this place...I cannot pronounce it. Are you a Norwegian?"

"I am lost too." Yes, he was drunk!

"Okay, where is your home?"

"I am lost," for the entire night as we walked he uttered this some 20 times. He was not that bad though, he had some 'Norwegian, Swede and Dane walked into a bar' jokes. The blizzard was beautifully playing along with our company for the night, calming itself down to listen more. The pines, the fjords and rorbuers listened to two lost wanderers talk about love, life, and Northern lights. We walked in ankle deep snow for 3 hours, until he finally sobered up and remembered that he forgot to ask "Do you remember your address though?"

I told him, and in half an hour, he dropped me off at my hotel. It was still dark, I insisted that he slept on the couch of my hotel room and he fell asleep like a baby. I did too, with a smile.

When I woke up, he was gone. I did not even bother to check if I had all my belongings in place. You might be wrong about someone you have known for years, but here is the thing – your heart always knows how it is going to end from the beginning! I knew he hadn't taken anything away. We would never meet each other again, I didn't take his contact information, but I took him for a dear friend and he did not disappoint! I just knew it.

The Red Rorbuers of Lofoten Islands

The World Outside is Worth Your Time, Go Out!

I have countless such stories and reasons to tell you that trust issues are stupid. As kids, we are told to not trust strangers. We are told to check for monsters everywhere before we can call it a night!

There are no monsters. Not below your beds, not out in the real world! We go out in the world, believing that something will hurt us and then it seems everything does.

There is good out there. It might not look like a lot, but there's enough. Humanity is very much still here. Kindness is alive and well, too. This world would have collapsed long ago if good had lost. It hasn't, and people everywhere save it.

We aren't as tough or as heartless as these rap songs would like us to be. We are vulnerable, at times helpless and most of the time, really hoping that Disney is based on real life. Travel makes you realize – it is!

What you send out- be it a fear or a deed, comes back for you! Find kindness in yourself and you will find it in foreign lands where apparently white people used to be racist. I am a brown girl and I was treated with waffles and hugs.

Our newspapers might tell us otherwise, but this world is largely good. I wish I could convince you that the two stories I shared are probably experiences of many, but you would have to see it for yourself.

Carry pepper spray, a knife or whatever voodoo that makes you feel safe; and come back home to realize you didn't even need to touch it once. The one thing you do need is intuition. If something about someone doesn't feel right, then chances are you aren't wrong! In the same village where I found the kind drunk man, I found another drunk man. On that very night! I met a Spanish man around 11PM, we got to talking and he offered me some drinks. I refused. Any woman in her right mind wouldn't go for drinks with someone she just met. He then expressed his interest in going for a Northern Lights hunt, and that being on my list too, I just tagged along.

However, somehow he picked up some 'signals' that were merely me being myself. I am giggly, jumpy, and always up for an adventure. He took it for flirting and when I revealed that I was not interested in him, he abandoned me at two in the morning. It was then that in the middle of the blizzard, I found my drunk Norwegian wizard. You know that story.

However, I would not remember that night or that island for someone who deserted me, but for someone who didn't. I did see the northern lights eventually, and when I did, all I could recall was my drunk friend telling me, "You know, in Norway, we like to think that Lady Aurora only dances when Gods are happy with us. Your Karma must be good for you to see it." Perhaps, it was…to have found such beautiful encounters.

As a woman who travels solo, we have our doubts. The world might raise its boys differently from its girls; but it has raised humans nonetheless. You will find great ones and some harsh ones, and they will leave you with memories. Some sweet, some bitter – but in the larger picture, all needed!

They say, a traveller can never be someone who is bitter at heart. Today, I can understand why. I have met so many beautiful souls while travelling, they all had different stories and reasons to travel.

A lot of them were travelling to fix their broken bits, or to escape sadness. Does it work? I think it does. "I started traveling when I broke up with my girlfriend, it was a 7-year long relationship. She cheated, I was heartbroken," I am sure you have heard this story before, but the man in question has travelled across 25 countries today. I met him in Nepal. He stays there now in a humble little hut that doesn't have space for furniture, but he looks content. He goes out daily to see the sunset by the mountains, teaches the kids of villagers, and when he has enough money, he buys chocolates for them and sometimes takes them on treks inside the Himalayas. Like I said, travel doesn't leave you a bitter person.

When you do it alone, you start valuing yourself. You start valuing life, not just yours, but other lives around you too. He has 3 pet chickens, 2 goats, and a bunch of parrots.

"I don't get it...if you don't cage your birds, how do they still come back to you again. This is a forest, they don't need to depend on you for food...then, why do they come back every single day? This is incredible loyalty!"

"No, this is love," he says. Life had come full circle for him. He found love and loyalty in his tryst with travel.

The people who say "nothing can fix you, but yourself" haven't travelled enough themselves to know that a journey is therapy. Somewhere in the middle of the journey, all your loose ends get back together.

There is so much for you to see, to know, to feel beyond the same old x; it might seem far, expensive or scary, but it is worth it. Every journey is worth it. Life, in my opinion, is itself a journey!

Yes, you have to look out for yourself. There will be times when you will be on your own. There will be bruises and wounds too. However, a lion would still choose to stay in the wild, rather than a cage! It's all safe there, but that's not where it wants to be.

Go out with hopes, not fears; like my mother says.

Akanksha Holani

Akanksha Holani is a part-time traveller and a full-time writer. Having worked with various established media houses for over 5 years now, her passion for wordplay has also become her profession. If she loves it, she has probably already written about it or is planning to, while booking the tickets to her next trip. She has worked really hard to make her phone gallery into "travel goals," yet ironically avoids Instagram!

Facebook: https://www.facebook.com/akanksha.holani
Linkedin: https://www.linkedin.com/in/akanksha-holani-92417197

From Suburbs to Sightseeing: One Woman's Road to Solo Travel

by Sarah Kilbourne

"Aren't you scared?" I frequently get asked this question when I tell people that I travel solo. If you had asked me ten years ago, I would have told you yes. Nowadays, I love solo travel and I often prefer to travel alone.

I want to share my travel experiences because I often get asked by other women how I started traveling alone and the conversation usually ends with them saying, "I wish I was that brave." I totally understand because I used to think like that too. When I was in college a friend told me her cousin had just spent a year in Australia and I started firing out questions like "How'd she get someone to go with her? She didn't? Did she have family there? No? Did she know *anyone* there? No? How did she go alone?!" I so badly dreamed of taking a year off to travel but was worried about *who* I could convince to do that with me. Did I know someone who was willing to quit their job and uproot their life like I was? I did in fact end up going to Australia for a year by myself, but it was not an overnight change.

Let's Start at the Beginning

I suppose I got the travel bug from my parents. As a kid, we would regularly spend Friday nights watching my parents' travel slides — yes, slides. They would set up the projector in the living room and we'd look at the slides they had taken from their travels around Europe and Asia. During the holiday season we'd travel to Montana where we spent Christmas at my grandmother's and then would drive down to Yellowstone and cross-country ski or go wolf spotting. Most of the time I had my nose stuck in the newest Harry Potter book. Summer vacations were spent hiking, backpacking, rafting, or canoe camping in places such as California, Idaho, Minnesota, Montana, and Washington. My brother and I had to beg for a "normal" vacation to Disney World. Through these intrepid adventures growing up, my parents instilled a sense of adventure in me from a young age. I just wish I had appreciated it more. I think I spent most of the time complaining about the long hikes and day dreaming of having a flying broomstick that would take me to a sunny beach. Typical kid.

The Author in California with Her Family, Circa 1996

Once I started high school, my family's travel destinations became further-reaching to places such as the Virgin Islands and Costa Rica. My mom encouraged me to go on school-sponsored educational spring break trips to Europe. By the time I graduated, I had traveled with classmates to six European countries on three different trips. These trips were fun, of course, but I spent less time soaking up the culture and more time goofing off with friends and taking advantage of the lax drinking age over there. We were young and of course enjoyed the attention from the young European guys we met, even with the language barrier. While at the Eiffel Tower, my friend and I started talking to two guys, neither of whom spoke English, but spoke French and Spanish. I spoke minimal French and she minimal Spanish, so the four of us were able to communicate in a roundabout manner using a mix of languages. These early brushes with travel laid the foundation for what was to come next.

When I entered university, I didn't hesitate to study abroad. I was a double major in French, so I wanted a program that would allow me to get French credits. My school didn't offer one, however, so I picked a third-party program where I was the only person from my college going. This was pretty intimidating for me since it was the first time I would be traveling to a foreign country by myself. I knew there would be other study abroad students when I got there, but I was still nervous. The night before I left was my friend's 21st birthday party and we all celebrated a little too hard. I woke up the day of my flight not having packed a single thing. Two of my friends came over to say goodbye and ended up helping me pack my bags; they talked me out of packing unnecessary items, like a five-pound French dictionary I thought I needed to bring with me. At the airport I panicked and bought an eighty-dollar watch since I didn't have any other way to tell time. Then I realized I hadn't told my bank I was leaving the country, so I logged onto a computer that charged by the minute to contact my bank. Meanwhile I heard the last call for boarding for my flight and almost forgot to log out of my expensive internet session. I ran onto the plane with only a few minutes to spare, sat down in my seat with my new overpriced watch, and started bawling my eyes out. My first solo travel experience was off to a great start.

Like I knew I would, I met other study abroad students in my program and made some good friends with whom I traveled to countries such as Spain, Germany, England, Ireland, and the Netherlands. One thing you may or may not know about France is that they love to go on strike. My friend and I booked train tickets to spend a weekend in Amsterdam, however, on the day we were supposed to leave, the train company canceled our departure. We hopped on a later one which was bursting at the seams with people from other canceled trains. By the time we got to Paris we had missed our connecting train to Amsterdam, so we were advised to board a train to Brussels that was leaving in five minutes. Without thinking it through, we hopped on the train relieved that we were at least making it closer that night and only needed to take a quick train in the morning. It quickly dawned on us that we needed to find accommodation. We didn't have smart phones, so we were texting our friends asking them to look up hostels for us. The only ones still available were crazy expensive and, being poor college students, we didn't want to pay for them. I texted a Belgian girl in my class to see if she could hook us up with a place to stay, but that proved unfruitful. We talked about sleeping in the train station or going clubbing until late and showing up right before the train. Unbeknownst to us, the two women next to us were American-a mother and her daughter-and had been listening to our dilemma.

As the train pulled into the station, the mother leaned over and told us she couldn't consciously let us sleep in the train station since it was dangerous. They offered us a place to sleep on their hotel room floor if we couldn't find anything else, which we ended up doing. See, there's still nice people out there! We got up around 3:30 AM to get to the train station to catch our final train, only to be kicked off at the next stop because of a ticketing miscommunication. We waited another hour in the Rotterdam train station before we finally got the train to Amsterdam and had a 24-hour whirlwind excursion. I got a lot more out of that weekend than I bargained for, and I learned that traveling in France keeps you on your toes.

    I had a blast during my semester abroad, and as my return to the US loomed closer, I was looking forward to being home for Christmas, but also was dreading leaving. As it turns out, I almost didn't make it home for Christmas due to a massive snowstorm that shut down London's airports and almost did the same to Paris. The day we were meant to fly out, our first plane was canceled due to the storm, so we were re-booked for the next day. The first flight was yet again canceled the following day, but we had decided to skip that flight and take the train to Paris in hopes of getting on my connecting flight back to the US. Upon arrival in Paris I was told I no longer had a guaranteed seat and I was on the waiting list. The two friends I was with rushed off to their flight and texted me they had made it before taking off. I felt crushed because we had made a plan to spend Christmas in Belgium together if none of us could get a flight out in time, and now they were on the way back to the States while I awaited my fate at the gate. Hundreds of passengers had been stranded in the airport for days, sleeping on yoga mats while trying to get flights home. I started crying at the thought of spending Christmas alone in an airport in a foreign country. After many hours passed, a gate agent showed up and told those of us who had been standing in line for an hour to sit down because the wait list was chosen at random. As the flight started boarding every second seemed to drag on as other passengers from the waitlist got called up to the flight. My heart sank deeper and deeper as more minutes passed and I imagined what my lonely Christmas sleeping on a yoga mat in the airport was going to look like. Finally, I heard my name called and I rushed up to get my ticket. I cried (again) as I called my mom, who was also crying, overjoyed that I was actually making it home two days before Christmas.

Avoiding the Rat Race

I returned from study abroad and graduated from college the following year. I had been daydreaming of ways to return to France, but I was also caught up in the hustle of graduate-college-and-immediately-find-a-job mentality. I landed an internship at a major public relations firm for the summer and was feeling stuck between two worlds; did I want to do what I had grown up thinking I needed to do and work a traditional 9-5 job? Or did I want to go against everything I'd been taught about what it meant to be successful and travel instead? The internship was a good learning experience; I learned that I didn't want to work a 9-5 job, not yet anyway. The world of interns was a cutthroat one, full of people bidding to get hired full-time. I was at a big company and the work I did went unnoticed - just a cog in the machine one might say. This all left me feeling uninspired.

I decided that before I could commit to a career, I wanted to see what other opportunities were out there. I had heard about a program through the French embassy that hires Americans to be English assistants in French elementary, middle, and high schools. I applied and got accepted, and I didn't have to think twice about taking the job. I was placed in a small town I'd never heard of before called Dax and was worried I was going to be the only assistant there. On top of that, someone I'd met over the summer had heard of Dax but told me it was terrible and that I should live in Biarritz and commute, which would entail a three hour journey each day. I stressed endlessly before leaving... "Where am I going to live? Am I going to meet people? What am I doing!?"

I arrived in Dax, finding the sun shining brilliantly on a charming French town. A quietly-flowing river cut through the town as the sound of pedestrians chattering and cars zipping by filled the air. I learned that this was a town that was famous for its thermal waters, which many people frequented for healing purposes. "This will be just fine," I thought to myself. That first day while wandering around town I found a coffee shop that sold frappés with such delightful ingredients as Nutella and Kinder Bueno. My friends and I would eventually frequent this place at least twice a week throughout the year. I decided to live in the dorm suggested (but not paid for) by the program and found that it wasn't a dorm at all really, but a neat little studio with a kitchenette and private bathroom. I was the first assistant to arrive, but by the end of the week there were eight of us all together.

Those seven months of teaching were filled with challenges, such as kids using the class as an excuse to goof off, not being taken seriously since I was younger than the "real" teachers, and learning to navigate the French language in real life as opposed to in a classroom setting. However, the year was also filled with amazing memories of biking through the town to the aforementioned coffee shop with my fellow teachers, visiting wineries and small French towns, and of course making great friends that I still keep in touch with six years later (we reunited back in France two years ago!). You can bet I took advantage of how easy it is to travel around Europe during my time there. My parents came to visit and we went to the Czech Republic, Croatia and Italy. Various friends from college flew over to visit and I met them in countries such as Spain, Italy, Portugal, and Turkey.

I decided seven months wasn't enough time in France, so after the teaching gig ended, I found a family looking for an au pair (live-in nanny) in a small seaside town in the southwest. I spent four months of the summer and fall taking care of two adorable French boys. During my free time I went to the beach, learned to surf, biked around the pine forests, and traveled by myself to San Sebastián across the border in Spain. I met a great group of other au pairs and dated a French guy for a couple months. My parents visited again, this time with my aunt, and we explored what seemed like endless charming countryside towns. I had a blast, needless to say. Before returning to the States I squeezed in one more trip to the UK. I spent Thanksgiving in

London with friends, got to visit two of my new friends from teaching who were back living in England, and then spent an awesome week and a half touring around Scotland on my own. I booked a group tour through the highlands, which was a great way to meet other travelers.

I can't say how glad I am that I took this opportunity and sailed away from the safe harbor, as Mark Twain would say. Those 15 months have had a lasting impact on my life; I discovered new things about myself, I matured in some ways but not in others, I traveled alone, I made friends, I partied too much, I made mistakes, I put myself out there, I got hurt, but I didn't let anything stop me.

Heading Down Under

Living abroad had given me a taste of what was out there beyond the US borders and I was hungry for more. After spending nine months saving up money by waitressing and living with my parents, I set off once again. This time, however, I was completely on my own. There was no program I would be working for, no housing arranged, no one that I knew except for a friend from college and a couple people I had met during previous travels. I was off to Australia on a working holiday visa!

This visa allows you to spend up to one year living and working in Australia, but how you go about it is completely on you. There are services out there who, for a hefty fee, will help organize job interviews and maybe housing upon arrival, but that's not what I wanted. I wanted to do it on my own. My friend from college picked me up at the airport in Sydney and let me crash at her place for the first week I arrived. This definitely helped to cushion the blow of arriving in a new country where I could count the number of people I knew on one hand. I spent two weeks in Sydney before deciding I didn't want to get stuck there for my whole year and left to go up the coast. A friend who I had met in Scotland asked if I was interested in au pairing for her friend's brother. Initially I wasn't too keen on au pairing again, but it was work and included free accommodation, so I went up to meet the family and really liked them. The family lived in Brisbane and had an adorable 18-month old daughter. I only worked two days a week, but I picked up waitressing jobs on the side. I joined an outdoor adventure group that organized activities such as kayaking, wakeboarding, and trips to nearby islands. I was part of a French conversation group. I volunteered with a nonprofit group that was fighting the good fight to protect Australia's marine environments. I spent my first Christmas away from home and in a hot environment, which was a double whammy. I traveled to Tasmania with other backpackers I met online, and we spent New Year's Eve on a deserted beach far from the city with a big box of wine.

 I uprooted from Brisbane and traveled for around five months, spending time in New Zealand with college friends and traipsing around Australia. My parents came to visit and we hopped around the continent like kangaroos (sorry, had to say it). I took the train clear across the country where there was nothing but red sand for miles and maybe a sheep or two. I volunteered for two weeks at a wildlife refuge inhabited by wild dolphins and met a park ranger who told me about another marine project she had worked on in Mexico. I immediately emailed the director and started making plans for my next adventure. Meanwhile, I went on a road trip up the western coast and across to Darwin with a friend in one of those giant caravans you only see old people driving. It was a unique experience. I ventured on alone to Alice Springs where I spent two weeks, which was "far too long" according to people who had never been there. I dug my toes into the red sand, learned to paint in the aboriginal style, and made some good friends.

When I was running low on money, I found a job back on the east coast in the backpacker town of Airlie Beach. It was a fun two months of living with coworkers who became friends, cleaning boats for extra money, partying until late some nights, while lounging on the couch in front of the tv for hours other nights. Just before my year was up, I got my open water scuba diving certification all because my mom had encouraged me to try diving when I thought it was something I wasn't going to like. It's all about trying new things, people!

It was during this year that I realized I wasn't going to be happy sitting in cubicles working for a public relations firm representing clients that I didn't believe in. I don't think I quite knew what direction I was heading in, but I had found my next move: Baja, Mexico.

South of the Border

Of course, a girl's gotta work before jaunting off to Mexico, so I was back with my parents (bless them) for four months to save up money. At the start of the new year in 2016, I headed once again to an unknown place by myself, but this time with an organization welcoming me into their arms. So what was I going to be doing you ask? Oh, researching whale sharks. YEAH. These animals are freaking beautiful. I will admit before going to Australia I had no idea what whale sharks were, #fail. In making plans to travel up the west coast of Oz, I had heard about them and my friend and I decided to book a tour to snorkel with these majestic fish. I loved it so much that I signed on with this nonprofit in Mexico to be a whale shark volunteer for two and a half months. As a volunteer I helped collect data on the sharks, meaning I was swimming with them taking photos of injuries or watching their behavior. Back in the office, we would enter this information into spreadsheets and databases. We had a software program that could recognize a shark based on its spots, which are their version of fingerprints, so we were able to track how often we had seen that shark before. On any given week we would take the boat out three to four times, sometimes with paying guests to introduce them to our ecotourism gig, and sometimes just to do research. The point of the research was to help one of the directors with his PhD research, but also to compile the data at the end of each season and turn it into the Mexican government in the hopes that they would enforce regulations for the protection of this species.

Mexico, 2016

The organization is based in La Paz, Mexico which is a nice little slice of paradise in southern Baja. I fostered a street dog while I was there and he joined me on activities such as biking, walking, and longboarding around town, as well as stand up paddle boarding in the bay and searching for the best tacos in town. He even came whale sharkin' on the boat with us once, but he got seasick, so we didn't bring him again. I also took Spanish lessons, got my advanced scuba certification, and learned the basics of freediving.

Wanting to take advantage of being closer to South America and visit a new continent, I flew down to Chile, which was deceivingly further from Mexico than it looks on a map. My friend and I backpacked in Patagonia, which was indescribably beautiful, and to this day one of my favorite places I've ever been. Afterwards I met my parents in Peru and we trekked to Machu Picchu and then traipsed up to Ecuador to visit the Galápagos

Islands, which is-as I'm sure you've heard-a fantastic and magical place. I hit up Colombia before leaving the continent, but to be perfectly honest I was feeling homesick and ended up cutting my trip short by two weeks. I was surprised by this feeling of homesickness, as I'd spent longer stretches of time out of the US before. Sometimes these things happen and you just have to do what's going to make you happy. For me that meant flying home early. I wish it didn't happen while I was in Colombia because I'd been so excited to go there and ended up missing out on a lot - but hey, just an excuse to go back, right?

A Tourist in My Own Country

Whilst galivanting around South America, I had applied for and landed a gig with a tour company back home that lead cross-country road trips around the States. Not long after I returned from my travels I was off again on another adventure. I spent three weeks training with a group of goofballs who are kindred-wandering-vagrant-spirits before we were unleashed on our own to take groups of Brits and other Europeans or Australians around that big beautiful country of mine. The first trip was terrifying but I ended up surviving and led three other tours that summer and had a pretty darn good time doing it. I got to see a lot of places that I'd never been before like the Grand Canyon and Zion National Park. That summer reminded me that there is so much to see in my own country. I had been so focused on running away from the States to other continents that I forgot how much I love my own.

Utah, May 2017

That winter I decided I was going to do something I'd been dreaming of for a while: work a ski season. I think I buckled into my first pair of skis around 5 years old and I've been snowboarding since I was 10. I started applying to different resorts in Colorado and Wyoming and reached out to a couple friends who I knew either had worked or still worked in ski towns. I chose to work at Crested Butte mostly because the start date was after Thanksgiving, which is one of my favorite holidays, and I had missed the occasion in years past due to being overseas. I knew one person who lived in Crested Butte- a friend from high school- and she was a great resource in helping me find a job and tips on housing, but other than that I was on my own again. In such a small town it was pretty easy to make friends, especially when you work on the mountain. I had a pretty breezy gig at an outdoor bar situated part way up the mountain, and the office views were hard to beat! I ended up getting a second job at a restaurant in the next town over and spent my winter working, riding, and playing. That season was a great snow season and there seemed to be fresh powder practically every other day.

I had a bad breakup towards the end of the season but had already bought flights to Europe to visit my now-ex. My mom suggested still using the ticket to go somewhere else and I started researching places to go. Unconsciously I was looking at all exotic locales since I had just spent the past four months in endless feet of snow. I remembered people raving about Nicaragua and less than an hour later I had changed my ticket to go there. I was excited to travel solo again and during this trip I met many like-minded people and tried a lot of new things. Some of the highlights were boarding down the side of a volcano and scuba diving at night amongst bioluminescence.

Nicaragua, April 2017

On the Road Again

That summer I signed on for a second season of tour guiding, which was even better than the first since I knew what I was doing. I led some awesome trips, such as a national parks trip in Utah and one that went up the west coast, into Canada and across the country, eventually ending a month later on the east coast. I spent my birthday with one of the groups in Monument Valley, sleeping under the stars and listening to wild horses gallop around.

I took the month of July off and visited a country I'd long been dreaming of: Canada. I planned this trip with the same friends I traveled New Zealand with. We flew into Calgary, rented a car, and ventured up to Banff. We did two backpacking trips, one of which included a thrilling and terrifying encounter with a grizzly. I used to make fun of Canada, but I never will again because they have nice people and even nicer scenery. That's probably why they just go along with us Americans making fun of them because they know they have it so good up there. After my friends flew home, I lingered in the country to visit British Columbia and see friends I had made from tour guiding and traveling. I topped the trip off with a visit to Washington State to see family and more friends, and boy, is there some beautiful scenery out there. I understand why everyone is flocking to Seattle.

The Harsh Continent

I had met a fellow tour guide my first year who was about to embark on a season of working down in Antarctica. As an avid wanderluster, visiting the coldest, driest continent had been something I'd fantasized about ever since I knew what Antarctica was. I kept in close contact with my friend throughout the year, and by close contact I mean I pestered her every other day to ask what the chances were that she could hook me up with a job. And my girl came through. She put me in touch with her boss and I was offered a contract to work as a driver.

I took off for the ice continent not having any idea what to expect, only knowing that I was excited to go. It's so hard to describe this place accurately to someone who hasn't been there. I worked as a contractor at the biggest science station on the continent and while I had envisioned spending four months being isolated and living out of a tent in the middle of nowhere, it was nothing like that. I found an amazing community of people at the bottom of the world who mostly all led vagrant lifestyles like myself. If you thought I had an interesting life, you should meet some of these people. There were people who worked as mountain guides on Denali, people who were building a robot for the exploration of one of Jupiter's moons, as well as people who explored the deepest caves in Mexico. It was a diverse group. Surprisingly, there was a lot to do in Antarctica. There was a yoga class almost every day, a craft room, three bars, three gyms, a cat club, a French club, a band room and endless landscapes of snow and mountains. It was an awesome four months, but by the end I was ready to leave and see trees again. I traveled, mostly solo, for a month in Cambodia, which led me to getting involved with this book.

Antarctica, October 2017

Enjoying the Aloneness

Okay by now you get it, I travel a lot. My point is that every experience I've had has somehow or another led me to the next chapter of my life. I think this has everything to do with me being open to new opportunities and not being afraid to go out and travel on my own.

There were many things that made me nervous about the thought of traveling alone before I started doing it; I didn't want to have to navigate foreign cities or countries by myself, I didn't want to ride on public transport in said cities or countries by myself, I didn't want to have to eat meals by myself, and I didn't want to stay in hostels by myself. This even translated over to being in the US where I wouldn't want to do things alone. Humans inherently don't want to be alone, we like being surrounded by other people. But I couldn't always find people who wanted to go where I wanted to go, or more importantly, people who could go for as long as I wanted to. I decided I wasn't going to wait around for anyone else to start traveling. If I wanted to go somewhere, I was just going to go on my own.

Once I started traveling alone in other countries, I found myself being more independent back home, too. I used to feel self-conscious doing things by alone, but I don't think twice about it now; I enjoy going out to eat alone, going to the movies alone, and hiking alone.

Being Accommodating

Where do I stay when I travel, you ask? My obvious choice is a hostel. The unrealistic and, in my opinion, corny movie *Hostel* gave hostels worldwide a bad reputation, but they aren't anything like the fake Eastern European one in the movie. They are clean, economical, and serve as a great way to meet other travelers. Most have private rooms, female only dorms (which I tend to choose), and coed dorms. I use the site Hostelworld to find places to stay, since they have a loyal user base that adds honest reviews and ratings of the hostels.

Despite what the movie *Hostel* may lead you to believe, hostels aren't scary. Strange things do happen there sometimes, however, like the time I woke up in the middle of the night in a Dublin hostel because a drunk Dutch guy in the same room mistook my bed for his and decided he didn't care that someone was already in it so he laid down the opposite direction and passed out. Most people tend to choose the bottom bunks at hostels, but I would first make sure you're not sleeping under someone who has bed wetting issues while inebriated. On that same trip to Ireland, one of my friends got so drunk on his birthday that he peed through the mattress onto our friend who was sleeping below. She woke up to the dripping from above and quickly figured out what happened, and of course was totally disgusted. She showered and spent the rest of the night on the lounge couch, much to the dismay of the hostel staff.

I also like to use Airbnb for accommodation. I typically don't use this while traveling solo because often it's more expensive than a hostel. However, it is a good option to use when traveling with friends. Airbnb has the option of renting a private room in someone's house, which is great if you don't want to stay in a hostel, but don't want to stay in a hotel either. If you're in a larger group, you can rent out an entire place. Airbnb gives the added bonus of a local perspective and if you're lucky the host may offer to take you around.

I have tried Couchsurfing once and I was apprehensive because of the stories you sometimes hear about it, but it was actually a really great experience. My host picked me up at the train station, we ordered pizza and I fell asleep watching Indiana Jones. Even though he left the following morning for a trip, I was deemed trustworthy enough to stay a second night and had the house to myself. I would advise exercising caution and making sure you stay with a host who is verified and has a plethora of positive reviews from female travelers, which is how I chose my host.

I've slept in cars a handful of times while traveling, but I wouldn't recommend it. It's usually been cramped and humid, which resulted in a terrible night's sleep. I did this in Munich during Oktoberfest because we had planned our travel so last minute everything within 30 miles of the city was sold out. In Tasmania when I rented a car with four other backpackers, two of the nights we all tried sleeping in the car to avoid camping fees. Let me tell you, it's worth it to spend the money on a bed at a hostel or at least a campsite to lay down.

Final Thoughts

I think one of the most common misconceptions about traveling solo is that you are always alone. I constantly find myself surrounded by other travelers, often other solo travelers, whether it's on a plane, bus, or at the hostel. I'd say that it's less about traveling alone, and more that you're not traveling with people that you already know. In fact, one of my favorite things about traveling solo is that you are forcing yourself to go outside of your comfort zone and talk to people you wouldn't talk to if you were with friends. You often end up meeting really interesting people, whether it's the locals in the country you're visiting or the other travelers you're meeting along the way.

Another thing I enjoy a lot about traveling solo is that you have the liberty to decide what you want to do and when you want to do it. You don't have to wait around for anyone else to wake up and get ready in the morning to go sightsee. You don't have to make compromises with friends about what you want to do. You are the only person you have to worry about.

Most of my solo travel experience is abroad but traveling solo doesn't necessarily equate to traveling solo abroad. I initially only wanted to travel and live abroad. You couldn't have paid me to live in the US and I was so sure I was going to settle in a foreign country. It was when I started the tour guiding gig, a job that I got because of my travel experience, that I realized how much I enjoy my own country and how much there is to see here. This doesn't mean that I don't still enjoy traveling abroad, but I'm taking the time to discover everything there is to offer in my home country instead of avoiding it like I used to.

For many, the first solo travel experience may be an international trip that they've been dreaming about for ages. For others, the idea of leaving the country alone can be daunting and that is totally fine. Traveling solo within your own country could be a great gateway to going abroad after you've gotten a feel for traveling alone. The important thing is just to start somewhere.

To be completely transparent, traveling isn't all sunshine and rainbows like you see on Instagram, but that of course is part of the adventure. I've had plenty of mishaps throughout my travels, like when I got altitude sickness hiking the Inca trail, or when I smashed my camper rental into the roof of a gas station in Australia and had to pay the employee $50 to fix it, or when I was in Rome with my parents and my mom got her purse ripped out of her hands by some guys on a moped. For every inevitable con there is to traveling, there are at least twice as many pros. I've swam with whale sharks in two different oceans, I've watched the embers of a bonfire burn in the wee hours of the morning on a French beach, I've jumped into freezing glacial lakes in Chile and I've rung in the New Year in complete daylight in Antarctica.

Travel has changed my life for the better and had I not been open to traveling solo I might not have ended up where I am now. Through traveling, I figured out what it is that really matters to me and what I want to do with my life. I don't dare to imagine where I would be if I hadn't had the courage to take off on my own and follow my heart doing what I wanted to do.

You're never too old to travel alone and it's never too late to start. But why put off for later what you can do now? Get out there and explore this awesome Earth that we are lucky enough to call home.

My advice to you is to not live your life according to someone else's standards of happiness. There is not one definition of success. My definition is as long as I'm happy, I consider that successful. Life is too short to be miserable. Get out there. Discover the world.

Sarah Kilbourne

Originally from Virginia, Sarah has been living a semi-nomadic lifestyle ever since graduating college, trying to figure out what this crazy world is all about. She's visited over 40 countries, over 40 states, and has been to 6 of the 7 continents. Sarah recently completed her first thru-hike, walking close to 500 miles on the Colorado Trail. Besides hiking and traveling, Sarah's hobbies include scuba diving, seeking out French people to practice her language skills, and looking at pictures of red pandas on the internet (they're so cute!). She is currently living the seasonal rat lifestyle, which she thinks is pretty darn good. Sarah is either somewhere in the mountains or daydreaming about being somewhere in the mountains.

The Travelling Sarcastic Goes Solo

by Daisy Busker

Daisy, 47 countries and counting.

Gain Confidence While Exploring

As much as I agree that it would be cliché to say that travelling changed my life, it really did. Travelling gave me the confidence that I never had growing up, it makes me feel as if no mountain is too high and as if there is a destined path out there for me to explore as long as I keep an open mind. My name is Daisy, a 25-year-old blondie from a tiny town in the Netherlands and this is my story.

Maldives, Photo Credit: Naomi Busker

I grew up in a small village in a small country, close to Amsterdam and the airport. Back then I always loved to guess where all the planes came from and where they would travel to next. However, I never felt the urge to get on a plane myself. I have a massive fear of flying and even now, after boarding over 300 planes, I still don't feel at ease in the high skies. I know, trust issues and all, but I do understand how to control my fears now after all this time. I had never been on a plane before the age of 17, nor left Europe. I travelled, mind you, but within Europe. We often ventured out in the Netherlands, Germany, Austria, France and even Spain. The distances here are different from the United States as Paris is just a 4-hour drive away from my house.

The urge to travel did not really develop until I reached the age of 16; I just about graduated high school and it was my dream to go to the US and experience high school there, mainly so I could go to prom like all of my favorite TV-stars did on the Disney channel. But I realized that it would be highly unlikely that I would get asked out by Zac Efron for prom and started to seriously look into colleges here that would allow me to study-or take an internship abroad. During the summer that I turned 18 I enrolled in a program for the summer in California; it was an English course and travel at the same time. I was incredibly nervous, my second time on a plane and there I was, on an 11-hour flight by myself to a country I had never been before. By the time I landed in Los Angeles I had already swam back home four times in my head and was nowhere close to being excited for the adventure. However, I got picked up by my host-mum who would take me in and care for me while I was studying. She fortunately was the nicest lady and made me believe that even though I was thousands of miles away from my comfort zone, I could still feel at home.

During those two weeks I made friends in no time and they had all different kinds of backgrounds and nationalities. We learned how to speak English together while travelling in California. When we took a weekend trip to Disneyland in LA, I realized that I never before had been this happy without any of my friends or family members. I learned that I enjoyed being on my own and getting to know myself. As much as I dreaded going on this trip weeks before leaving, I hated leaving the States even more. This trip defined the new me that was going to college and I came back a new person.

High school and college are tough enough as it is and, especially as a girl, you are being scrutinized for every outfit choice, decision, and your group of friends. I never was a member of the well-known popular girls, and I will be the first to admit that I really wanted to be one. I guess I always imagined them to be fearless and confident. Travelling gave me that feeling without having to change myself. Being abroad on your own is just about as far as you can get from your comfort-zone and during that summer I learned that one can gain confidence without being one of the popular girls.

Moscow, St Basil's Cathedral

Those two weeks changed me and my life in a way that I could never have anticipated beforehand. After coming back home, I couldn't stop thinking about my next destination. Luckily my program in university allowed me to travel to Russia and experience the city of Moscow. Boy did I fall in love with this city. The beautiful architecture, churches, metro stations, and monuments that are widespread across the city. Absolutely stunning. But moreover, I was fascinated with the culture and Russian language. It made me realize that you can travel to the other side of the world to find a building that you had seen on Instagram before, but the intangible things truly create the journey. Due to this experience and realization I had made up my mind, I needed to explore more and learn about myself away from home.

Life Changes Whether You Want It or Not

I had just turned twenty years old and entered my third year of university. Because my university program included three foreign languages, we had to take an internship and a semester abroad in order to learn one of the three languages properly. I chose French, English and German, and moved to Germany first to complete my internship for a marketing firm. I was stoked to learn how to speak German fluently, plus it wasn't too far from home. Even though I was excited, I was also incredibly nervous about moving out and being on my own. In the Netherlands I still lived at home and it would be the first time that I would have to take care of everything myself. Therefore, I chose to move to Düsseldorf, a big German city close to the Dutch border, far but not too far.

During these 5 months I learned how to fully take care of myself, do my own cooking, cleaning, laundry, and have a full-time job. I can honestly say that I had to grow the hell up, and fast. It was one of the toughest times for me as I also learned new bits about my personality that I wish I could change. But being on my own allowed me to handle that by myself away from those that already knew me well. Furthermore, it taught me how to be strong and take critique.

After being away for 5 months I found out that my father had stage four cancer and that he wouldn't be around for much longer. Never before had I felt this helpless and alone. There I was, away from home with news that changed my life for the worse. Therefore, I chose to move back home and be around family. Being away from those you love makes you appreciate them even more and realize just how much happiness you can gain from being around positive and like-minded souls. Had I not been away before, I might never have had the courage to go abroad again as I would always fear that something would happen to my loved ones. Moving out taught me that being away doesn't mean you lose those you love, in some ways it might even bring you closer to them. I quickly realized that being home with family was just what I needed. The urge to travel would always be there, but my father would not.

True Friendship Isn't About Who You Have Known the Longest

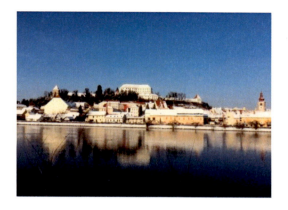

Slovenia

As all my classmates went abroad for a semester, I stayed home and took a minor in sustainable and economic development. Even though it wasn't necessarily what I wanted to do, I did enjoy being home and making memories with the family. Furthermore, I decided to take little weekend trips to see my classmates abroad and still get a little taste of the experience. During one of those trips I met my best friend. We both came to Slovenia to see friends that studied there, and it turned out that our friends knew each other. We bonded over drinks and mutual weirdness and have been best friends ever since. So, I guess you could say that aside from confidence, travelling made me meet my best friend and I still am grateful for that. Together we have now travelled to 10 countries and have experienced some of the craziest things.

One of those trips took us to South Africa, and gosh what a country. Backpacking there is truly amazing. We started in Johannesburg, and being that it isn't the safest city, we decided to take a tour. The tour took us to some of the most beautiful places I have ever seen; a gorgeous camp set up in the middle of Kruger Wildlife Park, a bright milky way, a burning campfire and a glass of South African wine. We saw the big five on safari, took bushwalks, and woke up to animal noises, something both scary and thrilling. Yeah, those five days were pretty incredible. After our safari we decided to take on Cape Town and the Garden route. Our hostel in the city provided a first-class view of Table Mountain and was located right in the clubbing street of Cape Town. The next day we took a van across to the most southern tip of the African mainland and standing there literally makes you feel as if you could fall off the earth at any moment. The rough sea with its sky-high waves, filled with sharks mind you, truly took my breath away.

South Africa, Kruger National Park

Be Fearless

Another bucket list experience for me would be bungee jumping. Bungee jumping is one of these things that you always mention as a once in a lifetime opportunity, and I was no different. When we were given the option to jump down 281 meters, the world's highest bungee, I straightaway said yes, and cried internally. Gosh, I didn't dare to eat breakfast nor look down when the moment to jump was there. Yet, the countdown 3,2,1, bungee and the music got me so hyped that I jumped before 1. It truly was one of the most terrifying things I have ever done but also one of the most freeing. It took about 6-8 seconds till the first bounce back up and about 3 minutes to be back on the platform. While jumping I was scared but looking back on the experience I would do it again in a heartbeat. Sometimes I re-watch the video to remind myself that you have to take a chance every once in a while. My friend and I still look back on that jump as one of the coolest things that we could ever have done together.

Another beautiful thing about South Africa is the fact that it has a suitable climate for vineyards and wineries are open every day for tastings. Sippin' wine while overlooking a stunning vineyard anyone? Often you can pair the wines with cheeses and chocolates. I've never felt as satisfied in my life as I was here. South Africa will forever hold a dear place in my heart and I can truly recommend going there to anyone. A word of advice, though, be cautious and careful when there and take a tour into consideration when travelling alone. They allow you to meet new people and go places you otherwise may have missed out on.

Grief, British Weather and Moving Abroad

After my trip to South Africa, my father passed away and I had no clue what to do with myself. I was lost and drowning in grief. It was always my dream to study abroad at a university and my father had encouraged that. Therefore, I chose to enroll in a master program in London. Again, far enough to be on my own but close enough to go home for a few days. Looking back at this choice I was running away from mourning and nowhere near ready to be on my own. I guess that I always imagined that travelling would keep me going and that the urge to explore would always be there. That year taught me differently. I didn't really want to be there nor did I open up to anyone to try and make friends. I fully focused on graduating university and making my dad proud even though he would never see me graduate. With that in mind I kept on going and one year later I received my diploma and officially could call myself a lawyer in maritime law. Though I was happy and proud of myself I didn't feel the amount of joy that I had hoped to feel.

While living in London I tried to experience as much as I could in terms of living in such a massive city. In Holland I lived in a tiny town with just 500 inhabitants. My apartment complex in London housed over 800 students; imagine the shock I went through. I rented out a small studio in Greenwich, a gorgeous part of London which is often used as the backdrop for movies, such as Bridget Jones and Thor. I felt like a woman of the world when I ate lunch by the riverbank overlooking the Thames River while waiting for my next class. One can easily get lost in such a massive city, just its metro system can throw you off in seconds. But being anonymous has its advantages and it allows you to be on your own.

Tower Bridge, London, UK

Funnily enough I learned that I wouldn't want to live in a big city forever, I missed the fresh and crisp air of the countryside and being able to just drive anywhere easily. Furthermore, being dependent on public transport proved to be a big challenge for me. Back home I had a car and being able to plan your own schedule works differently when you have a bus schedule to keep in mind. For someone who often is late to appointments that is one big adjustment. However, I made contacts easily, way quicker than one would on the countryside. Apps such as bumble-bff, tinder, and certain Facebook-groups allow you to easily meet others that are looking to meet new people near you. It was with those people I got to explore the fun and quirky bars that London has to offer. Such as the Saturday markets at Camden lock and the local comedy nights. With three other students studying abroad, I took a spontaneous trip to Prague and that somehow ended up as a portrayal of the Hangover movie series. We went on a pub crawl with a massive group and somehow, after some liquor, I got ordained online and led the ceremony of two of my travel buddies that decided to get married on the spot. Overlooking the river, we laughed, had more wine and then got escorted away in a police car. Yes, that's right, they spent their first night as a married couple in jail. What had happened was a random stranger harassed us, which led us to calling the emergency help line, but due to the language barrier they misunderstood us, and we got taken to the station as well. Scary at the time, yet a great story now.

During my time in London I learned how to connect with strangers and how to have small talk. I had always been a social person but too shy to put myself out there. Being on my own required me to do the one thing that I feared the most: open up to others. Considering that my father had just passed away I didn't really feel like doing so. Therefore, I made contacts but didn't really allow myself to build strong friendships since I was, and still am, healing. Even though the experience in London wasn't what I hoped it to be, I still am glad to have experienced it. I learned things about myself and about life that I otherwise would never have.

Road Trip Anyone?

I love road trips, words can't describe just how much. During the summer after university I went to the USA and mapped out a route that would take me to over 25 states. My mother, sister and I rented a RV and took the interstate headed south from Washington DC. One of our first stops was Rodanthe in North Carolina. A cute little town on the coast, well known for the Nicholas Sparks movie Nights in Rodanthe with Richard Gere. What a place, colored beach houses, little restaurants and beaches for miles. If I had to move anywhere in the states, that would be my go-to location. After that we took on the cities of New Orleans and Chicago which in my opinion are way cooler than the better-known cities like LA and NYC. We ended our trip in the national parks of the west. One of our goals was to see a bear in the wild and boy did we. When we checked in to our campground in the north of Minnesota the manager told us to be cautious with garbage as they had a bit of a "bear situation." Meaning that bears roamed the grounds looking for food. Being from a country where the red fox is the largest mammal around, we were on edge but excited at the possibility of seeing a wild bear. Bloody tourists, I know. When we walked around the campground at dusk, we heard a noise not too far behind us and freaked a little. There it was, a large black bear picking food from the bins. With an uncanny flexibility he opened the massive lid and grabbed 2 full sized bags which he would run off with in just a matter of seconds. Truly one of my favorite memories, which was enhanced by a bald eagle soaring past us the next morning.

Minnesota, USA

After coming back from the states, I decided to experience nature in its purest form by going to the Arctic. I got a job volunteering at a husky farm in northern Finland and was I excited. Dogs, snowmobiles and the northern lights, what more can you ask for? Maybe some heat, as -40 degrees Celsius was more crisp air than I had asked for, but let's not be difficult now. Every morning the other international volunteers and I woke up to 70 Siberian huskies howling for action and food. We suited up in about 5 layers and started to harness the dogs that were selected for safaris or training that day. Words can't describe the feeling of soaring through the frozen tundra on a sled pulled by 4-6 huskies in complete silence. I learned how to live and sort of survive in the wilderness, nowhere near Bear Grylls, but hey that is a start. Every week the dogs ran 5 km further than the week before, which made the rides extra-long. After those runs, we would feed the dogs, often in the dark with headlights on as daylight is limited to 4 hours a day during the winter months. At night we often saw the northern lights, or Aurora Borealis, dancing above our heads. That phenomenon makes you feel as if you are a part of a greater plan in the universe. Seeing the bright colors and trying to photograph them well is just incredible. You have to be very lucky to see them but when you do, life is just complete.

Kemi, Finland

Getting Ready to Sweat Down Under

After those three months it was time to move to Australia, from one side of the globe to another. From -40 to +45 in just a week's time. Sweat had gotten a whole new meaning to me during those first few days in the land down under. In my opinion, Australia is one of those places where everyone can feel at ease. It truly has such a relaxed vibe to it and the beaches and beautiful weather only contribute to that. Together with my mum and sis we traveled across the country to experience as much as we could. During our three months we roamed from the rainforest in Queensland to the outback to the aboriginal culture in the Northern territory. Every day had been an adventure. Some of my favorite memories were made in Queensland, more specifically Burleigh Heads. In my opinion it doesn't get more Aussie than that. Surfers with beach bods and hair anywhere, hipster food, and more lovely locals than tourists. The beach overlooks the skyline of the Gold Coast but doesn't have the crowds or outrageous prices. Somehow, I can imagine myself living there forever, with year-round summer and sunshine. During our time there, the northern tip of the state was struck by hurricane Debbie. Being that we were in the south we didn't get more than heavy rain and strong winds. We had planned a trip to the Whitsundays shortly after and were surprised and shocked to see the aftermath of such a natural event. I guess that being from the Netherlands kind of makes you immune to heavy rain but seeing this was totally different and heartbreaking at the same time. Even one month after the hurricane the waters of the great barrier reef were still cloudy. Nonetheless we had an incredible time and the Whitsunday Islands are breathtakingly gorgeous. Plus, who hasn't got snorkeling/scuba diving in the great barrier reef on their bucket list?!

Hill Inlet, Whitsunday Island

Australia is also known for the Outback and experiencing a few days there is highly recommended. Therefore, we embarked on a plane to the red centre, Ayers Rock also better known as Uluru. When I thought of Australia, that was one of the first things to come to mind. Seeing the sunset over the enormous rock is incredible, the change of colors and the bright red clouds around it is just amazing. Our tour provided champagne and nibbles so just imagine my excitement. The day after we hiked through Kata Tjuta National Park, a place with stunning rock formations and climbing over rocks all day. I was so tired I didn't even notice the freezing cold temperatures at night when sleeping in a swag. The biggest struggle was yet to come when hiking through King's Canyon the next day. The first part of that hike is called heart attack hill and I quickly figured out why. Stairmaster is not able to prep you for that. But once at the top, the views are worth every drop of sweat, plus you can eat a bar of chocolate guilt free after. Make that two bars actually. The canyon bears resemblance to the north rim of the Grand Canyon but much smaller. At the bottom of the canyon there is a sanctuary called the "Garden of Eden," a beautiful serene location in the midst of nowhere. This sanctuary is an absolute must visit when in the park. That night we camped out on a cattle farm with no other humans for miles. Just camels and cattle. The bathroom did not even have a door so that was one visit to remember.

Rottnest Island is one of those places that one only recognizes based on the locals, which in this case are furry and cute as hell. Quokkas are little kangaroo/guinea pig/bunny-like mammals that only live on this island. Over the last few years they have gained more popularity due to the so-called Quokka selfie. These little animals are harmless and super friendly, which is why many people flock to the island to see the crazy critters and snap a pic or two. We named ours Quinten the Quokka and he is the reason why I prefer them over kangaroos. The island itself is stunning; crystal-clear water, a pink lake and beaches everywhere. It is very small which makes it an ideal weekend getaway from Perth.

Nanny Life Isn't Too Bad

After three awesome months, my mom and sis had to go back home for work and college, but I really didn't want to leave Australia and decided to look for a job in Melbourne. I had only visited the city for a day and really wanted to explore more. Online I found out that a lot of families hire au pairs in the city. An au pair is basically a live-in nanny, often from abroad to contribute to a cultural exchange. Via Facebook and agencies, you can easily find families that are looking to hire an au pair. Fairly quickly I got a message from my future host-mum. The conversation flowed really well and I felt a connection with the family straight away. The family has three amazing boys. They grew up having au pairs caring for them, which is great as they were super helpful showing me around. My duties included cooking, cleaning, taking the boys to sports and school and helping them with homework. The boys are obsessed with food so cooking skills were required, these kids could eat. We often played soccer, cricket, and swam in the pool together which was good fun. I had never played cricket before, but with them teaching me I could finally understand the game, and even played a little. The amount of energy those boys had was contagious and I felt like a member of the family. Their home was located 20 minutes outside of the CBD in Melbourne, in one of the family suburbs. Therefore, there were multiple other au pairs around to meet.

Through Facebook groups regarding au pairs in Melbourne, I quickly set up a couple coffee dates with fellow au pairs. My first "date" was with Nicole, she is from the UK and lived 2 blocks away from me, I don't know why but I was super nervous. However, we sat down in a cute little coffee place and got chatting straight away. Luckily, she had been in Melbourne for a couple of months and wanted to show me around and help me get started. We clicked really well and she truly has become one of my closest friends today. During my first weekend in the city I met up with Alicia and Emma from Luxembourg and Canada. We went out for drinks in the city and had an incredible time on Chapel Street. Memories were made that night that we still refer to today. Nicole already knew some other au pairs in the city and set up a little lunch date in Brighton for us all to meet. Together with Emma and Alicia we met up with Nicole, Charlotte from the USA and Malin from Sweden. We went to one of my favorite places in Melbourne, the bathing boxes. Brightly colored beach boxes right on the beach, which provide a great view of the city skyline. The six of us clicked really well and chatted as if we had known each other for years.

 I remember leaving to pick up the boys from school realizing that I had truly found my home away from home. We tried to meet up for lunches, nights out, tequila Thursdays, weekend trips and movie nights as often as we could. Melbourne has a lot of cute little bars and Insta-worthy restaurants. Our favorite place to go dance was Georges Bar, a cool bar in Fitzroy. Great music and a low-key vibe, gosh words can't describe how much I miss this place.

Shrine of Remembrance, Melbourne, Australia. Photo Credit: Naomi Busker

One of my favorite memories is Oktober festival on the beach. It was Malin's birthday and we decided to celebrate at the festival in the traditional dirndl dresses. A full day of good music, drinks and celebration in tiny dresses. It doesn't get much better than that. Another memorable day was the day of the Melbourne Cup, the horse races. People go all out with their outfits and the event is massive. We had bought cute dresses, high heels and hats in order to fit in like locals. It turned out to be gorgeous weather and with the drinks flowing we had a great day, which ended early in the morning in the city. Even now that we are all back home again we still talk on a daily basis. Malin even came to see me a couple weeks ago in Amsterdam, catching up and exploring the city was amazing. Plus, a trip to Paris is on the books in a month's time to see the others.

Being that there are so many au pairs in Melbourne it is easy to meet others. Two of them being Emmaray and Kat from the States. We bonded over our mutual love for food and exploring, which is why we took a spontaneous trip to Sydney. We checked into the hostel and, after exploring the sights, we ended up at the opera bar underneath the Sydney Opera House. One of the most scenic wines I have ever had. Sydney is much more status oriented than Melbourne and everyone really dresses up for a night out, meaning high heels and dresses. Being that we were backpackers, we felt kind of out of place but that only contributed to the girls' trip atmosphere. We danced the weekend away and chilled on Bondi beach afterwards. That weekend proved to me that you don't have to know each other for years to establish a bond that will last a lifetime. We snapchat daily and call once every month at least. I feel really blessed to have met such incredible girls from all over the world who will forever be in my heart, and that would never have happened if I hadn't put myself out there in Melbourne. Getting out of your comfort zone and opening up to others is as scary as it gets but these girls are the living proof that it is totally worth it.

During my last week in Melbourne I was emotional as I really didn't want to leave the life that I had built there behind. It felt perfect, great group of friends, family and routine. The girls organized a lovely goodbye party for me with a brunch by the pool and a big night out. I cried my eyes out saying goodbye to these treasures. We had become incredibly close and it felt as if I was leaving my sisters. Plus saying goodbye to "my boys"; these three little boys had made such an impact on my life, whereas they might not remember all that much of me while growing up. I was never sure about having children later on, but they showed me that I do want kids one day if it's in the cards for me. Luckily my host mum keeps me updated on their lives, that way I can still see them grow up into the awesome teenagers and men they are destined to become. Plus, I hope that they will come to Europe one day and let me show them around the child approved sights of Amsterdam and the Netherlands.

My solo move to Melbourne made me feel incredibly empowered and wanting to travel solo. I have moved long-term to many places but actual solo travel I had never dared to do. People always found that fact very funny as I seemed so fearless, yet I was uncomfortable with the idea of getting out there on my own with just a backpack and camera. Therefore, I decided to take a small group tour by myself in Western Australia. The tour would take me from Perth up to Exmouth on the Ningaloo reef in the north to snorkel with turtles and manta rays. Again, I was nervous about walking into a hostel by myself and meeting others, which is crazy as I am social and talk to anyone. I felt really alone. However, my roommates were incredibly kind and the tour would depart in the early morning. Our tour group consisted of 8 girls and 2 guys. Everyone was chatty and we all had different stories and backgrounds to discuss. We went sandboarding, hiking and swimming, which was incredible. The highlight of the tour consisted of snorkeling on the Ningaloo reef. Less coral than the Great Barrier Reef but the turtle, manta ray, and shark sightings made up for it. The manta rays especially were amazing to see as they are about 2-4 meters wide and just glide through the water like a leaf in the wind. I had never felt so small in the ocean before. Those 12 days made me realize that backpacking by myself wouldn't be scary at all and that it is really easy to meet others as long as you are open to it. That realization made me confident for my next adventure, backpacking in Asia.

One Trip Leads to Another

While being in Melbourne I started playing with the idea of going backpacking in Asia after I had to leave Australia. Two of my friends in Melbourne, who happen to be Dutch as well, had the same idea. We started to map out a route that would take us to as many places as possible while still being able to relax. As one of them planned on going to New Zealand beforehand, the two of us would start our travels together and we could meet up in Thailand after one month. Dana and I met four months before we would start travelling together, but we clicked straight from when we first met up for lunch. We decided to start our trip in Singapore, a metropole in chaotic Asia. While in the city, it is only the unbearable heat that reminds you that you are in fact in Asia. It is one of the cleanest and most well-organized places I have ever been. Great food and everyone speaks proper English.

From there we hopped on a flight to Bali, Indonesia. I had been there before and was excited to go there again with a friend. We found a cheap resort with a pool and after our busy nanny days we wanted to relax a little and sip on a cocktail or two. Bali is pretty touristy and one really has to search for authentic Indonesian culture. The temples on the island are stunning nonetheless and we rented a car to explore as many as possible during one day. My favorite has to be the water temple on the northeast side of the island. Since it is further out of the tourist beach towns, very few people actually make it out that far. The temple is placed in a manmade lake which is filled with large koi fish. The area feels serene and quiet, which makes it a little hidden gem midst the hustle of the island. The rice terrace fields in this area are also less crowded and just as beautiful as those that are more well-known. After Bali we went on to the Gili Islands which have some of the most idyllic photo ops there are. The sunset side of the islands has numerous sets of swings just on the edge of the water. Providing you with the perfect photo sitting on a swing above the turquoise sea. Furthermore, it is one of the best party spots in the country and there are parties on Gili T every night. While we were there, we met a couple who told us about the beauty of Myanmar. This country has opened their borders for tourism about eight years ago which means that the experience there is more authentic than Thailand, for example. Kids are still excited and shocked to see westerners and locals are more helpful and genuine. Due to their enthusiasm and the rainy weather in Indonesia we decided to book a last minute flight and go to Myanmar.

I loved this place. We traveled across the country by night bus mostly and rented mopeds to explore the many temples during the day. Bagan is absolutely one of my favorite places in the world. The area contains over 2000 temples, stupas and pagodas which makes it bloody easy to indulge in the beautiful sights. The best part has to be the sunrises. Every morning 25+ hot air balloons go up at sunrise and seeing those float above the temples is stunning. When you have got money to spend, definitely go for a ride yourself. We made the choice to go for it and I haven't looked back. It was the highlight of our trip and friendship.

Bagan, Myanmar. Photo Credit: Dana Coret

After Myanmar we agreed to meet up with Hester in Thailand to party hard on the island of Koh Phangan during the full moon party. This party is rumored and loved amongst the backpacker community and I can assure you that it is all true. It is one of the biggest parties I have ever been to. It has fire dancers, liquor from buckets, people that are drunk or high and most importantly great music on the beach. The days leading up to the actual full moon are filled with parties as well and I highly recommend being on the island a couple days in advance, as it gives you time to meet new people and experience the vibe on the island before the madness. We stayed in a party hostel and didn't have a dull moment. We didn't sleep for five days straight and I probably had more liquor than blood in my veins, but it was worth it. The pool parties are insane, and the beer-pong tournaments are more intense than the world cup. Everyone there comes to have a good time and we sure had one. I believe this madness is a once in a lifetime experience to have with so many new friends.

Number One Beach in the World

The full moon party was the end of my trip with Dana and Hester and I left to go to the Philippines while Dana headed back to Australia. The Philippines is one of those places that has gotten a bad reputation for travelling yet is home to the most beautiful beach in the world: Palawan. Therefore, I was eager to explore this place while I was near it. We landed on Cebu, one of the many islands of the Philippines. There we swam with whale sharks and turtles as well as jumped off of waterfalls at Kawasan. A super active and crazy week filled with experiences. Many countries in Asia have developed a transport company for the use of tourists, which often includes buses with aircon and locked bag storage. Here that wasn't the case and you are stuck in a crazy busy bus with your bags and sweat on a tiny seat for hours. Call it an experience if you want but I can laugh about it now. After Cebu we boarded yet another plane to Palawan. While there we met up with lots of people that we had seen before somewhere in Asia. As you will hopefully experience for yourself one day, everyone goes to the same places which makes it easy to find a travel buddy.

Palawan, Philippines

Palawan is a dream; turquoise waters, coral reefs, palm trees and small beautiful islands for as far as you can see. We went island-hopping on a relax and booze cruise. Seeing the sun drop behind the high cliffs was incredible. The downside to the authentic experience is that phones and ATMs don't really work there and you have to be more careful with ordering food as it is easy to get food-poisoning due to a lack of clean water and supplies. Yet that shouldn't stop you from going to this beautiful place as I had an incredible two weeks there. Food poisoning will hit you at one point during your travels no matter where you are. Just be careful with clean water and listen to your body.

Even though I had spent the last 5 weeks travelling with someone, I still ventured out on my own. Unfortunately, one of my friends got sick which left her unable to take tours for a couple days. When we first got to our hostel in Palawan I decided to sit down at a table and just start chatting to whoever sat down next to me. In a "normal" bar back home I wouldn't have the guts to do that, but in a hostel the rules are different. I had a great evening meeting lots of new people who would invite me to join their day plans. This made me even more comfortable for what was to come next, solo travelling in Cambodia.

I Do It Solo

Straight after arriving into Siem Reap Airport, I loved this country. Organized, sunny and good food. Plus, they used American dollars which makes it easy to convert currencies. I stayed at the White Rabbit Hostel, which is an Alice in Wonderland themed hostel with a pool and bar, just my kind of place. I straight away liked the place, quirky but not too much. My friend Dana set me up with a friend from back home who stayed at the same hostel. We got along really well and made plans to explore Angkor Wat over the next few days with some other backpackers from the hostel. If you are sarcastic and enjoy a drink then you are my kind of person. Cambodia has to have some of the most beautiful temples I have ever seen, you will need days to see everything and not get exhausted in the process. The best way to see everything is to hire a tuk tuk with a driver for the day, it allows you to cool off a bit and it is a must do in Asia. My two favorites have to be the Bayon temple and the Preah Khan temple. The first is one of the most visited places and very crowded, yet the amount of detail in the statues is incredible. Preah Khan is further out and therefore not as busy. The ruins are in some parts fully taken over by the roots of the trees which gives it a mysterious Jungle Book vibe. On one of the days Chelsey joined us and that is how we met. We never thought that we would end up writing a book together but again, that is the beauty of travel. Cambodia made be forget about my solo travel fears and got me excited about doing it more often.

Angkor Wat, Cambodia

My last stop in Asia was Kuala Lumpur, a giant city and nothing like the cities that I had spent the last couple weeks in. Fun and crazy into the madness again. The hostel had an infinity pool overlooking the city and the Petrona towers, I guess you can imagine where I spent most of my last days. My final night in Asia we went clubbing in one of the largest clubs in KL and we got a free upgrade to the VIP area and DJ booth. Funnily enough a Dutch DJ was playing that night, and we got to chatting a bit. From there it was time to fly home and reconnect with the place that I had left 17 months before. Coming home felt surreal, like I never left yet I wasn't the same anymore. I had been away from home for longer periods before, but I never felt this out of place. This time changed me for the better and I feared that I would return to old habits. I still miss travelling every day and I don't expect that to go away anytime soon. I miss the dynamic lifestyle and meeting a lot of new and diverse people. Yet I am grateful to have so many amazing people to come home to every time. Sharing your travel stories is half the fun and being able to show pictures and videos is incredible.

Want Some Advice?

Go out there and live a life you will remember. Great stories aren't told from a desk chair, but from a hammock overlooking the ocean. Travelling gave me more than a "serious" job ever could have at this age. I learned how to love myself even though there is plenty to be insecure about. Nobody is perfect, you will always find someone that you can connect with no matter where you are. And if you don't? Pack your bags and move on to the next destination. Why? You are the only person that can truly make you happy and satisfied.

Travelling gave me confidence, friends, love, stories and a life that I am proud of. Losing a parent at a young age makes you realize that life is meant to be lived, people will love you for it. My father always hated it when I went abroad. He wanted me to be his little girl forever, who would stay within arm length. Yet every day that I spent abroad he would message me saying that I shouldn't be homesick and that he loved me for not letting my fear of the unknown control my actions.

After coming back from that first trip from the States he mentioned to me how proud he was of me for following my dreams, no matter what society or someone else told me. Everyone needs to feel loved and wanted so I want to thank my support system for always encouraging me to get out there and do what makes me happy.

Some of my closest friends today I have met while on the road and they proved to me that you don't have to build a friendship for years to know that they will always be there for you, no matter where you might be on this crazy planet. Another thing that you will hear as a female solo traveler is: "but what if you fall in love and move there for good?" I don't know why, but somehow only women get this question. Well I can tell you this, I fell in love. Twice. And I still came back. To quote any tacky pop song: if it is meant to be, it will be. These guys were solo travelers like me who came into my life when I least expected. Though we separated due to different travel plans I don't regret meeting or leaving them. Falling in love is scary and even more so when you are on your own, yet the relationships you build are pure and genuine. Somehow it is easier too, no friends around to tell you that he isn't the one. Just you, him, a cider and a gorgeous sunset. Kind of feels like a three-star rated romcom but it was perfect.

Women Do It Better

Traveling solo as a woman is scary and a lot of people will tell you not to do it based on some kind of assumption. Yet here we are, nine kick ass women telling you that you can. Being afraid is human, but don't let it scare you from living the life that you want. Bad things can happen to you anywhere. And I am living proof, I have lost a parent, been pickpocketed, been stranded, cried myself to sleep because of homesickness, and ate my body weight in comfort food. Yet I am addicted to the feeling of excitement, possibilities, adventure, the unknown and most importantly to be open to anything. I can't go back to being the person that I was before, nor do I want to. You don't have to be fearless to be brave and all it takes is one brave choice to be hooked to travelling forever. Start with a small solo trip, even a weekend getaway will do. Just realizing that you can make all the choices yourself is enough, plan the trip fully based on your wishes rather than someone else's opinion. These little changes will help you develop and love yourself more. Every choice will lead to something bigger, just be open to it.

Thank you for taking the time to read my story, it hasn't been easy or without heartbreak but nothing ever is. That is the funny thing about this thing we call life, you just have to get up and live it. Thank you to everyone who has been a part of my travels, you know who you are, you have all changed me for the better and I wouldn't be me without you.

Love, Daisy. xx

Kuala Lumpur, Malaysia. Photo Credit: Melissa Meotti

Daisy Busker

My name is Daisy, a 25-year-old Dutchie with big dreams. I come from a small town just outside Amsterdam. I am blessed with the best family and (international) group of friends a girl could ask for; yet the urge to travel is always in the back of my mind.

After high school all I wanted to do was travel and see more of the world. With that and my business background in mind I enrolled in a bachelor's program called International Business and Languages. I completed this course and left to begin master's program in London. A year later I had successfully completed my LLM International and Commercial Law. Even after a year abroad I still wanted to learn so much more about myself away from home and my comfort zone. Somehow unplanned I have been travelling, working and living abroad on and off since the summer of 2016.

Travelling makes me feel alive in a way that I can't possibly put into words. Even though the past few years haven't been without obstacles, I wouldn't change them. The best part about travelling is the people that you meet along the way and seeing places you never imagined visiting before. Currently I am on a three-month backpacking trip through South America. At the time of writing this I am sippin a cocktail in Cartagena, Colombia and soon headed to Peru.

I can't make your decisions for you but what I can do is tell you that there is a world out there waiting for us females.

Curious about my travels? Follow me on Instagram: https://www.instagram.com/daisbusker

I Was Here

by Katie Birtles

I'm going to die, sitting in the middle of two strangers eating dry biscuits, staring at Kindle screens. I'm lifted out of my seat and my stomach lurches, rolling into my throat. Stifling a scream, I release a low groan instead. Oh my god. I'm going to die.

I've desperately nudged my neighbours aside, claiming the arms of the seat as my own. But my white knuckled grip is useless. We are about to go down and once we plunge, it's over. There's another sharp drop into gravity and I reach for a bag to hold over my mouth. Fucking hell, we are going to die.

Suddenly, a melodic voice cheerily echoes out, informing me that we are, in fact, not going to die. It was just a bit of turbulence. I decide that flying is not for me.

Hours before, I had been a big, tough girl, striding through the airport with a bursting suitcase and a boarding pass. I watched the people around me, wondering where they were going. Was it as badass as my trip? One way to Accra. A two-month trip. My first time travelling solo. All on my own.

My excitement and conviction had been palpable until it was time to go through customs and say my final goodbyes. I took one look at my mum silently weeping and burst into sobs. I was scared. What the fuck was I doing? My mum had pulled me into a hug and told me she was proud of me. I kissed her cheek and meekly walked through customs, tears tracking down my face.

I landed in Accra 24 hours later, dazed and exhausted. But as I walked through the airport with strange smells and sounds swirling through the air, I began to well up with the thrill of adventure. My stride was back.

The Decision

I'd always harboured a curiosity for faraway worlds. Growing up, my dream job changed often, but it always centred around travel. As a young girl, I imagined myself as a TV presenter travelling to exotic destinations. As a teenager, I wanted to be a cultural anthropologist, studying complex communities around the world. By the time I entered university, I wanted to be a foreign correspondent reporting in far-off locations and when I graduated, I wanted to work in international development.

My desire for adventure and exploration had always been more than just a dream or a vision for a short holiday. Travel was a major life goal, central to my growth, success, and contentment as an adult. When I began feeling restless and stagnant in my second year of university, I knew something had to change.

There wasn't anything wrong with my life, but it wasn't fulfilling either. I spent my days in a monotonous haze of study, small-town clubbing, casual admin work, and a long-term relationship. I was only 21 but I hadn't achieved anything remotely interesting and I felt my youth was wasting away with my comfortable, safe routine.

I was constantly dreaming without taking any action. I spent hours planning trips, itineraries, budgets, and bucket lists, trying to align these plans with my friends and boyfriend. But they either weren't interested or couldn't prioritise the time or the money. I was waiting for the day they'd change their minds or I'd meet the perfect travel partner.

Or, I could do it alone.

It sounds like the obvious solution, but to me it was a wayward, whimsical notion. I'd never done anything alone.

I was incredibly lucky to have grown up surrounded by a strong network of friends and family. With both parents and three siblings, my home was always warm and bustling. As I grew up, I leaned on my friends, walking to school and having classes together, then spending all afternoon messaging each other. We'd go to parties, movies, and sleepovers together. When we finished school, we started jobs and university together and when we went clubbing, we'd stand in line for the bathroom together. We became women, side by side.

As we began to define our paths, our ambitions soared in different directions. Some were focused on careers, others were in dedicated relationships, some were saving for house deposits, while others went to university.

I remained focused on travel and realised that while I was waiting for someone to accompany me, I was missing out on a world of opportunities. I wanted to interact with different cultures and immerse myself in their communities. I wanted to learn languages, try exotic food, explore man-made wonders and wake up in breathtaking landscapes. I wanted to be shocked.

So, I stopped waiting. I gathered a little grit and stifled my insecurities. And I did it alone.

Once I made the decision to embark on a long-term, international trip, my plans quickly turned to action. I knew I wanted to work or volunteer abroad and I knew I wanted to go away for a few months. I'd always dreamed of exploring the African continent. I was captured by the vast and vibrant cultures and I felt compelled to explore these communities first-hand. Plus, it was about as different from my hometown as you could get.

I chose Ghana, the country known as 'Africa for beginners' due to its stable democracy, fast-paced development, and friendly people. I arranged a two-month journalism internship at the Daily Graphic newspaper and a homestay in the capital city of Accra.

Buzzing with energy and anticipation, I renewed my passport, organised a visa and set about booking flights and vaccinations. I was brimming with to-do lists and poured over travel blogs, determined to be prepared. I felt confident, clear-headed and strong with decisiveness. And yet uncertainty still wormed through my mind.

First, I doubted my capabilities. How would I know what to do at the airport? Could I really work as a journalist? What if I didn't make any friends? What if I hated it? But all these doubts disintegrated with positive self-talk. I could ask someone for help. This was an opportunity to learn. I'm sure I'll make friends. If I truly hated it, I could just come back.

Then I worried about my relationship. My boyfriend was completely supportive of the trip, but I couldn't bear the thought of spending three months away when we'd barely spent a night apart in four years.

We ultimately broke up five months before my trip, for unrelated reasons. He was my first love and my first break-up. The end was soft and mournful, an ode to our fierce respect and affection for each other. For weeks, there were tears and anguish and yet, I felt a distinct sense of relief. I was free to go.

Finally, I was plagued with the doubts of friends and family. Almost every single person who heard about my trip told me I would be kidnapped, raped, murdered, or struck down with a fatal disease. Many were completely shocked that I would even consider the trip, especially as a solo woman. They thought I was crazy, reckless and naive.

When the 2014 Ebola outbreak in West Africa hit the news, my mum became adamant I wasn't going. The disease never crossed the borders of Ghana; however, it did spread to Italy, Spain, the United Kingdom and the

United States, which are considered 'safe and acceptable' countries to visit.

The negativity and misguided perceptions simply spurred my desire to go. I understood their worries and felt grateful for their concern, but I hadn't dived blindly into my decision. Instead of relying on hyper-negative media portrayals for information, I'd conducted my own extensive research into Ghana and safety for solo women. I was confident I would be okay.

But I wasn't just okay. I was in full bloom.

The First Solo Adventure

I was striding through the airport doors when a sweltering blast knocked me sideways. Horns blared as cars wrestled for space and taxi drivers swarmed, clamouring for passengers. Families wielded trolleys stacked with towers of luggage, hollering to stay together in the crush. The soggy heat wrapped around me as I joined the ranks of sweating faces.

I was out of my depth and grateful for my host, who had met me at the airport. I clung to him as he expertly maneuvered his way to a waiting vehicle. The doors slammed shut and I sank into the cocoon. As we trundled away, I pressed my face against the window, struck with childlike wonder. I was here.

The dusty streets were strewn with stalls of sweet fruits and smoky rice. Cars and trucks hurtled along the fractured roads, horns clanging. Stray dogs milled about and scrawny chickens scratched in the dirt. Crowds of people were illuminated by brightly coloured fabrics, moving along to an inborn beat.

An incredible energy hummed through the towns. Laughing children danced around old stereos, stomping to the thumping music. Preachers hollered through megaphones, blaring prayers to the masses. Babies were carried in snug slings on their mothers' backs. Beautiful women balanced enormous baskets on their head, hips swaying as they walked.

I was wildly fascinated, scrambling to capture every detail in my mind. And it was in this moment that I fell hopelessly in love with travel. I felt like a kid again.

Travel wipes away cynicism and apathy. It removes the past and the future and places you firmly in the present. It is the magic of discovery. Do you remember that giddy happiness you felt when you were a child, from something as simple as a trip to the beach, ice-cream at the pool, or Christmas Eve? When was the last time you truly felt wonder? That's what I felt.

I arrived at my host family's house, wide-eyed and bushy-tailed. I was introduced to my new Aunty and Uncle, and Akka, a kind woman who cooked for us. I also met Tara and Cassie, my roommates for the next two months. They were both interning at a human rights organisation and our work would often collaborate as I reported on their campaigns for the newspaper. We quickly became close friends and I'll always treasure the time we spent together.

We had no running water and sporadic electricity and learnt the art of cold bucket showers together. In the sticky afternoons, we would lie on our beds, sharing stories from our day. We'd have dinner together, trying the local dishes. We'd traverse markets, learning to haggle with the locals, and escape into air-conditioned cafes for ice-cream.

At night we would go out to clubs and bars, where we met travellers from all over the world. We learnt salsa dancing, went to local cooking classes, and watched the 2014 football World Cup in the streets. On weekends we would explore the country, taking long bus trips to hidden waterfalls and sleepy beachside villages. We supported each other through homesickness, culture shock and bad days. And we were always singing and laughing, infected with the Ghanaian energy.

Hiking through the Mountains of Ghana

During the week, I explored the communities of Accra as part of my work as a journalist. I visited schools, political events, disability centres, and orphanages, interviewing inspiring teachers and community leaders. One week, I was invited to learn about a grassroots microfinance program on the outskirts of Accra. Walking within the depths of a village, I was introduced to program participants, including small business owners and families.

I met a woman who ran a successful food stall and had become the breadwinner for her family. I sampled her juicy sugar cane, sharing it with a horde of shy, giggling children who had gathered in the street. I sat cross-legged in a shanty, listening to the story of a family who survived on a dollar a day.

As we entered a compound, a group of children cautiously peered at me. The leader of the pack, overcome by intrigue, crept toward me. She warily took my hand, holding our palms together, examining the differences in our skin. Enthralled and humbled, I stood very still, holding my breath.

She began to laugh and beckoned her friends to come and see for themselves. Despite our visual differences, our bodies were the same and I was deemed human. Kneeling, I allowed their inquisitive little hands to explore the texture of my hair and the shape of my pointy nose. I wore a smile plastered from ear to ear, my heart bursting.

I noticed a baby girl staring at me with wide, honeyed eyes. The adults watching our interaction were laughing, and my guide translated their conversation. I was the first white person the little girl had ever seen.

I smiled at her encouragingly. She abruptly turned and waddled back to the safety of her father's arms, where she took quick, curious peeks from under her eyelashes. It was as if she'd seen a ghost. In her eyes, I guess she had.

When I wasn't scouring the streets for stories, I worked in the newspaper's office in Accra. The commute to the city was an adventure in itself. I left home on foot, walking through the humming streets to the 'bus station,' where I would find the man yelling 'Circle, Circle, Circle!' I would bundle into his tro-tro, an old van fitted with wooden benches, and try to claim a seat by the window.

We would wait until the van was brimming with passengers, then take off toward the city. Once we arrived, I would walk to the next station to take another tro-tro which dropped me a few streets away from the office. The whole journey took nearly two hours, depending on weather and traffic.

The tro-tros would often break down, in which case we would all get out and patiently wait for another to pick us up. One morning, a section of the van floor fell out, and the driver's mate pulled it back in place as we ducked and weaved through blaring traffic. Collisions and traffic jams were daily occurrences and thunderstorms would regularly flood the streets bringing the whole operation to a halt. That was just life in Ghana and it was frustrating, charming, and humbling all at once.

Those commutes on the local public transport became an invaluable part of my time in Ghana. They taught me patience and understanding. I learnt how to slow down and take life less seriously. Mark Twain was absolutely right when he said, "Travel is fatal to prejudice, bigotry and narrow-mindedness." I shook off these restraints and shared in many beautiful interactions with my fellow passengers.

One morning, I had just arrived in the city. Melding into the rolling wave of bodies, I allowed the crush to toss me out of the bus. With my feet firmly squared, I tugged at my pants and sucked in a breath, preparing to manoeuvre across the road. Dodging puddles, potholes and traffic, my progress was curbed by a row of brash street hawkers, clamouring for the attention of the people passing by. They hissed and hollered, relentlessly reciting their wares and prices.

I often walked by this group and most days I simply smiled and shook my head to indicate I wasn't buying. But today I felt irritated and refused to look at them, wrenching my arm away from their outstretched hands.

"Hsssst! Obruni, obruni!"

"Hey you girl, slow down!"

"Come see, come buy!"

I huffed my way across the road, anxious to reach my destination. Suddenly, my path was blocked again. This time by a silent figure. A little girl, no more than three years old, looked up at me, her bony arms outstretched. This time, I did not look away and I did not wrench my arms away.

I looked into wild, wounded eyes, sunken into the shadows branded on her skin. She held up her arms, as a child does when they want to be picked up. This tiny body with those deep, searing eyes, swamping her stained face. This tiny body, wanting to be held. All the instincts in my body screamed at me to pick her up and carry her away.

"Hey, are you lost? Where's your mum?" I softly asked her. She said nothing, her dusty lips clamped shut. I glanced around, peering through the crowd rushing past us, trying to pinpoint someone watching us. I was afraid to pick her up, knowing that a nearby mugger would likely swoop in while I had my arms full. I was also hesitant to give her money, as it would go straight into the hands of the adult forcing her to beg on the street, perpetuating the cycle of abuse.

Instead, I knelt down to her level, trying to engage her, willing her to speak. "I'm sorry, I can't pick you up. Where is your mum?" I pleaded with her. She would not speak. Maybe she couldn't. I wanted to take her with me. I thought I could at least bathe her, feed her, and find some sort of care for her. I took a step and motioned for her to follow. She did not move.

I took a few more steps away. As the distance between us slowly grew, she suddenly snapped, springing back into the crowd. I watched her scrambling among bodies, her tiny figure dwarfed against the legs she navigated. Eventually, I lost sight of her.

I merged back into the crowd, chest aching, oblivious now to the world whisking around me.

That could have been me.

It was nothing but sheer luck that I was not born into the life of that girl. A stark sense of reality spewed through me. I thought back to the vendors I had so rudely brushed off earlier. I was arrogant to believe that my time was too important to spare a nod and a smile for someone else.

The only thing that separated me from anyone in this world was an uncontrollable speck of chance. That was it. I felt ashamed and humble. That day, I dissolved any grandiose notions of self-importance I had harboured and took my place as a mere speck in the universe.

The Move Abroad

Two years later, I graduated from university with a desire to work in international development, inspired by my trip to Ghana. I scored a three-month job coordinating volunteers in Sri Lanka, leaping at the opportunity to immerse myself in another corner of the world. I lived in Panadura, a beachside town just outside Colombo, managing volunteers with medical and care projects in hospitals and schools.

A typical day would begin with a volunteer meeting, where I would coordinate the schedule. I would accompany the volunteers to the local hospital where they separated into different wards to observe and learn about the Sri Lankan medical system. I saw many extraordinary things at the hospital but my favourite place was the maternity ward. I adored the little babies, bundled up by their resting mothers. One morning, I was privileged to witness the birth of the child, which brought me to tears from both terror and awe.

Following the Train Tracks in Ella, Sri Lanka

In the afternoons, we would go to the beach or the markets or get involved in some community work, such as a beach clean-up or English lessons. One day, I was supervising an English lesson at a community centre in Colombo. I wandered outside and saw some children playing in the street. Seeing me, they smiled shyly, hiding beneath their mothers' skirts.

I sat down nearby, and a little boy and girl ran over and sat beside me. The little boy began chatting away to me in Sinhalese, staring earnestly into my face. I replied in English, trying to express that I could not understand his bubbling language; however, he was too young to comprehend our communication barrier.

My Sri Lankan colleague approached us, amused at our attempts to converse in two different languages. "Did you hear what he just said?" my colleague asked me. I shook my head. "He called you Akka. It means big sister. It's a sign of respect." I was wildly charmed.

Later that day, the same boy gently took my hand, leading me to a sink. He needed help turning on the tap, so he could wash his hands. In return for the privilege of his respect, I now held the duty to care for this boy. He saw me as an elder, completely capable of providing him with the care he required. I was 24 at the time, but it was the first time in my life that I'd really felt like an adult.

After my contract ended, I travelled around Sri Lanka for a few weeks with Marit, a Dutch woman I'd worked with for the past three months. We went north to the untouched beaches of Trincomalee. I was battling food poisoning and Marit could barely walk with an infected toe and we relished the time to soak up the pristine sand and clear water.

As we recovered, we made our way to the south to mountainous Ella, a cool change from the searing Sri Lankan heat. While Marit nursed her injury, I spent my days in a romantic haze of train tracks, tea fields and misty mountains. We parted ways in Ella and I began my solo journey, taking a bus to Galle.

I was nervous without my travel partner, feeling wary and unsure of myself. I was running low on money and had booked the cheapest accommodation possible. I arrived to a dodgy hostel with no other women in sight. I went out during the day, trawling the towns and beaches. At night, I locked myself in my room, scared and lonely.

I could've easily changed my accommodation to stay at a social hostel, but I was exhausted after three months of round-the-clock work and frequent illness. Instead, I made the decision to return home, promising myself I would try solo travel again when I was better prepared, both physically and mentally.

The Big Leap

Fifteen months after my return from Sri Lanka, I was ready to jet off again. Over the past year, I had worked as a travel agent in Brisbane, reaping the travel perks. The year had been peppered with trips to Cairns, New Zealand, Peru and Indonesia and with each trip I found it harder to come home.

On Top of the World on Padar Island, Indonesia

I was discontent with my job. I knew it wasn't going to be a long-term career and I felt I'd come to a dead-end. I felt fidgety and directionless. I'd always wanted to embark on a long-term solo backpacking trip around the world, but jobs and relationships had always held me back. I now found myself single and in a non-committed job. What was stopping me? I went through all my objections, methodically finding solutions to each one:

Money. I needed to be financially secure before quitting my job to travel long-term, but I was in an unusually privileged position. I had no children, no debt, and no responsibilities. I'd recently began a side hustle as a freelance writer which brought in enough money to sustain a cheap lifestyle of hostels and street food in southeast Asia.

Possessions. I lived a minimalist lifestyle and everything I owned fit into my bedroom. It was easy to sell or donate anything that couldn't fit into my backpack. I lived in a share-house and wasn't on the lease, so I just had to give my housemates time to find a new roomie before I left.

Family and friends. I was missing Christmas with my family, the wedding of a friend and a bunch of birthdays and important events. It's hard to be so far from your loved ones on these special days but there's always Facetime for the lonely days.

Career. I'd never had a solid career plan and often found myself jumping between jobs and industries as I discovered my talents and interests. I'd always had a passion for writing and saw this as an opportunity to commit to becoming a full-time writer. (Since my departure, my travels have actually been an asset to my career prospects.)

I was self-sufficient and more confident than ever. So that was that. I quit my job and set off with a backpack and a one-way flight to Penang, Malaysia. I chose Penang simply because I scored a cheap flight and it seemed like a good place to start. I planned to explore the whole of southeast Asia at my whim; no itinerary and no timeframe.

I spent a couple of weeks in Malaysia, traversing Penang, the Cameron Highlands and Kuala Lumpur. Mostly, I ate and walked. I would walk for hours, admiring the architecture and street art, stopping in at food stalls and bakeries to try new delicacies. I took time to ruminate and reflect on the pieces of my life.

I often met people who could not understand why I would choose to travel alone. Many people often assume that those who travel solo for a long period of time are running away from something, like a bad breakup or family problems. That can be true. But I wasn't running away from my problems; I was running away from their version of 'real life,' and running towards a world of adventure, freedom, people, places and experiences. I was barreling head-first into a life I truly wanted to live.

After Malaysia, I moved on to Bali, Indonesia where I settled in a hostel in Canggu. I slept in a room with a bunch of solo, long-term travellers and we became friends, bonding over our similar circumstances. We would work together on our laptops in cafes and get beers on the beach while we admired the sunset. We'd dance away the night in bars and kiss strangers in swimming pools.

I was the passenger in two scooter accidents in those weeks. I was incredibly lucky to come out of both with only minor injuries. I crushed my leg and struggled to walk but I refused to slow down and take care of myself.

Feeling restless, I moved on to Thailand. I met some old friends for a few nights in Bangkok before taking an overnight train and ferry to the islands. I settled on Koh Phangan, notorious for its full moon party culture. I spent a few weeks limping forlornly through boat parties and jungle raves until I found myself alone on a beach on New Year's Eve.

Earlier that day, I'd taken a hair-raising boat ride to the other side of the island. Carving our way through the churning waves, the little boat slapped up and down at an alarming angle. We bashed around clumsily as we held on for dear life, while the crew whooped and laughed as they danced over each bulging wave.

The ocean spat us into a small cove. I walked up the shoreline and arrived to a mass of shimmering, fluorescent humans. I watched as half the crowd lurched furiously to the techno music, while the other dazed faces swayed mystically to their own rhythm. It was a three-day island rave of the bright and bizarre, where the music never stops and no one sleeps.

I instantly felt lonely. I didn't want to be there, or anywhere. I felt lost, but I didn't know what I was looking for. I was in control of my surroundings, but I felt enslaved to my emotions.

Detaching from the throng of people, I followed a sandy path to the top of a hill. Descending the steep bank, I wandered onto a secluded beach, marked only by a small bungalow. It was empty and I felt relieved. I laid down to watch the sky shift to a blanket of stars, falling asleep to the waves lapping gently at the shore.

I woke to the sound of fireworks, feeling obliged to join the party and celebrate the New Year surrounded by people. Instead, I leaned into my loneliness, accepting the emotion. I stayed with myself until sunrise, watching the stars sink behind a curtain of brilliant pink rays. With the sun flexing high in the sky, I was ready to go.

As I walked back to the main beach, I collected two other solo travellers, a Dutch boy and an American girl who were both fed up with the party and were looking for an escape. We found a boat and made it back to the mainland, where we spent the next few days exploring together. As my loneliness subsided, I felt ready to move on and we parted ways.

People often think that travelling solo means you will always be alone. They're afraid of loneliness and boredom. I was too. But solo travel allows you to connect with yourself and the world in an intimate way. It challenges you to find peace with your own company and will expose you to a world of human interaction.

When you travel with friends, you always have someone to cling to. Solo travel rips away that safety net. It makes you far more open to initiating conversations and making new friends. It teaches you to cope on your own, but it also shows you that it's okay to need people too. Ultimately, solo travel gives you the opportunity to find joy in human interaction and the choice to entwine this with solitude.

Feeling refreshed, I took a ferry to Koh Tao to recuperate and allow my injuries to heal. I went snorkelling, kayaking and meditated at sunset atop the highest peaks on the island. I began to feel a sense of peace flowing through my veins and I knew I was on the right path.

Looking Out Over Koh Tao, Thailand

The Meeting

My Thai visa was coming to an end and I had to make the decision to extend my visa for another month or move to another country. I decided to travel to Myanmar. I wanted to get away from the hoards of tourists, oversized cocktails and fluoro singlets and explore an untouched corner of Asia. I'd read that Myanmar was unspoilt by mass tourism, retaining its traditions and authentic charm.

I once heard that we make 35,000 decisions every day. Most of these decisions are inconsequential. For example, I woke up one familiar, fuzzy day and made the innocuous decision to spend two nights in Bangkok instead of one (before I flew to Myanmar). So, I had to leave Koh Tao a day earlier. Then I chose to leave on the 1pm ferry instead of the 3pm and then I decided to catch the train instead of the bus.

These were all monotonous decisions, made only with the intention of getting me from one destination to the next, but I felt good after making them, if only because it feels good to cross a task off your list of things to do. But when I think about it now, I wonder if I felt so content with those decisions, because I was aligning with some ethereal plan, a vaporous nudge designed to move me into place.

Was I unknowingly conspiring to meet him when I made those decisions?

On the day I left the island, an invisible engineer had willed my decisions so that I was led to a seat on the ferry pier right around midday. And he, in his own celestial sketch of movements, had been steered into the seat right across from mine, right around midday.

We started talking on the pier, then after catching the ferry, we continued talking on the bus to the train station. We had dinner with his friends, then waited on the train platform. He checked my ticket and stopped me from getting on the wrong train, then we swapped numbers and waved goodbye.

He decided to stay in Bangkok and on my last night, I met him and his friends at their hostel. We had drinks, then moved on for dinner. We went out with the aim of finding a nightclub, but spent most of the night talking and dancing through the streets.

As the night wore on, we began to move into a bubble, leaving no room for anyone else. We made the excuse to go to the convenience store to get water and snacks and finally we were alone. We started walking, at first with a purpose, but then simply because we didn't want to stop.

We were moving along that wispy Bangkok street, when we came to a corner. He looked at me and it was his hand that was drawing me towards him, but it was his eyes that were pulling me, and they were the last thing I saw before his lips were on mine.

We kept walking, begging the night to go on. We talked about whatever we talked about, and he was entertaining and enthralling. But was it our words that kept us moving, or was it something unspoken? Because it was 5am and I should have been exhausted but I wasn't. I could see the first rays of light kissing the horizon, but it felt as though it would hurt if we had to say goodbye in that moment.

We held on to time as we ducked into a hotel, sewing up the space between us for the last few hours. Then it was truly morning and I had a plane to catch. We said goodbye. I barely had time to shower and pack my bag before I was taking off to another country.

I landed in Myanmar dizzy with travel romance. Travel can tear you from people as quickly as it pulls you together and I had to accept that I would probably never see that man again. I didn't know it then, but a few months later we would be together. Right now, I needed to withdraw from my world and immerse myself in the life of the country I was visiting.

I set off to Bagan, which remains one of the most extraordinary towns I have ever visited. It's an ancient landscape cloaked in gilded pagodas and mystical stupas. It felt like I'd stepped back in time as horses and carts clopped down the wide dusty roads.

I got chatting with a local artist who sold paintings for a living. I asked him about the best places to view the sunrise and we set off on his scooter to find his secret viewpoint. We weaved through fields of wildflowers until we stopped at a discreet temple. Ducking through the doorway, he revealed a hidden entrance to a stairwell. Sliding into the cramped space, I clambered up the dark passage until I saw a glimmering opening.

I poked my head into daylight, climbing onto the roof of the temple. The view was breathtaking. I stood still for a few minutes, turning slowly to take in every angle across Bagan. I thanked the man profusely for his kindness and made some notes to find my way back to the temple.

The next morning, I set off before sunrise to find the temple and after an hour of wrong turns in the dark, I stumbled across it. I was the only one there. Sunrise is a huge event in Bagan, with the best viewing spots always overrun with tourists. To have this incredible viewpoint all to myself was an absolute treasure.

I sat quietly and observed. The vast plains were a mismatch of palm trees, farm fields and pagodas, and yet not a single element seemed out of place. Bells tolled in the distance as sun rays began to yawn over the horizon.

The town was blanketed in a reverie, an awed hush. It roared around me, whipping at the hairs on my neck. This moment was not for speaking. Not for moving. It was not to be captured on camera. Such a fluid, slipping moment, cannot be set into time. It can only be felt.

A huddle of bulbs shrouded in mist, appeared on the horizon. Their fires flickered, boosting them higher and higher over the plains. Floating slowly and gracefully, the balloons melded into the dusty pink sky.

You can feel the tension building. Birds are cooing, flitting about in anticipation. The sky glows deeper. And suddenly it appears.

A startling red arch glides out of the earth, exploding in a blaze of colours. The hot air balloons and temple spires are a human touch in this parade of nature, but their silhouettes bask naturally in the golden rays. It is an act of harmony between the sheer magnificence of nature and the human ode to it. I break my gaze to wipe my eyes.

I am here.

The Magical Bagan Sunrise

The Reason

Before you set off on your own solo adventure, I need to warn you; solo travel is not for everyone. It seems glamorous and dreamy on Instagram, but the reality is that it can be downright awful.

You may be confronted with language barriers, loneliness, thefts, transport delays and having nowhere to stay. You'll often have to say painful goodbyes to new friends. I've faced fears, illness, accidents and assaults. You can march the whole world alone and yet you'll still need your mum when you're laid up in bed with food poisoning.

And yet, I can't stay still. Despite all the difficulties, solo travel has gifted me so much more.

It's the foundation of my independence and freedom, making me stronger, smarter and self-aware. It's bestowed me with gratitude, showing me that experiences are more important than things and time is more valuable than money.

It's boosted my problem-solving and decision-making skills, allowing me to face uncertainty with confidence. It's lead to career opportunities and beautiful relationships and has become integral to my identity and the mark I want to leave on the world.

When I wander, I am filled with fearlessness and a roaring energy. It thrills me and challenges me. It tests me, provokes me, double dares me. It forces me to truly observe and reflect. And of all these encounters, adventures, and confrontations, it has done only one permanent thing: broadened my mind.

If you want to flourish in your life, I implore you to get uncomfortable. Resist complacency and go in search of the unknown. Do not consistently lean on familiarity and routine and avoid the easy, well-worn path. Always take the challenge; if it scares you but excites you at the same time, *do it*.

Travel is a privilege and I've been more privileged than most. I possess the ability to work and earn money. I am healthy and able-bodied, with few responsibilities. I have an Australian passport. And I've always had a home to come back to if things really went wrong.

But you don't have to go on an expensive world trip to reap the benefits of travel. You could take a train interstate. You could explore a nearby neighbourhood. You could taste a new cuisine or talk to someone from a different culture. Chase that childish sense of wonder and revel in discovery. Albert Einstein said, "When you stop learning you start dying" and travel is one of the greatest teachers of all.

There is a force deep within my nature, that inspires me to discover and set down ribbons of my being throughout the world. I yearn to learn, share and impart experiences, knowledge, beliefs and emotions. Through every ridge and rivulet of our planet, and through every smile and wrinkle of its people, there is infinite wisdom and adventure. It is ours to seek, and endure, and adore.

And that is why I cannot stay still.

Katie Birtles

Katie is a freelance writer travelling the world.

Originally from Australia, she has lived and worked in six cities across 3 continents and has travelled solo through five continents.

She's written for bestselling authors, top podcast hosts and elite entrepreneurs, and currently lives in Bangkok working as a travel writer (her dream job)!

Katie's current adventure wish list includes a road trip through Eastern Europe, an overland adventure from Chile to Mexico, a rail journey from Russia to China, and a gorilla trek in Uganda. In the meantime, she also wants to continue that backpacking trip around southeast Asia.

And she still doesn't like flying.

You can follow Katie on her travels on Instagram: www.instagram.com/katiearoundtheworld
For professional enquiries email: kjbirtles@gmail.com

Thinking Outside the Box

by Chelsey Schultz

Solo Travel Thwarted

Flashback to 12-year-old Chelsey who asked her parents if she could go to Ghana to teach English. Her parents agreed as long as they could join. When they found out that the trip was going to be longer than a week, actually 5 weeks, they said they couldn't miss that much work. So, aspiring 12-year-old Chelsey asked if she could go alone. She received an instant "no" because "it was too dangerous." Her solo travel hopes were thwarted...

Flashback to 19-year-old Chelsey, who hopes to study abroad in Spain for a semester while at university. Chelsey has everything ready to go, all she has left to do is buy a plane ticket. Then she gets sick... So sick that she ends up needing surgery, but the doctors don't know when that surgery will be. Study abroad is canceled, and her solo travel hopes are again thwarted because now it is medically too dangerous for her to leave.

Flashback to 21-year-old Chelsey. She has completed university and offers to drive her parents' car across the country since they wanted it to be at their new home. Chelsey had it all planned out. She was so excited at the idea of taking a couple weeks to see her friends along the way and stop at some places she has never been. Yet again, the parents said that it would be too dangerous for her to drive across the country by herself. Even though Chelsey traveled for two months with a friend in Europe. Three times now her solo travel plans have been thwarted.

Flash forward to 22-year-old Chelsey. She is an adult, no longer under the thumb of watchful, but well-meaning, parents. She now has the right to pick her own path and choose what she wants to be. Those dreams of traveling solo, living free and alone never died. The naysayers and the disappointment of being thwarted again and again have not kept her down. She is ready to step out on her own.

A Bright New Day

This is where I was last year; having just graduated university and traveled with a friend throughout Europe. Jaunting through eleven different countries solidified my desire to see more of the world, to learn more about myself and what I wanted to be. I was ready to go beyond the box that I had been stuck, no longer trapped by the expectations that were set for me.

So, I signed up to teach English as a foreign language. I got certified with my TEFL degree, got a job, said goodbye to family and moved to South Korea in just a few months. Everyone was shocked that I was leaving so quickly, but I knew that if I stayed longer I would grow roots and become embedded in a life there. I did not want that life. I did not want to wait for my dreams to come to me. I wanted to get up and chase after them. That is exactly what I did.

When I moved to South Korea I was completely alone. I did not know the language, the customs, or literally anything at all. I had no friends and no family. The only thing I had was my job and the home that they provided me. I was petrified in the week gearing up to my departure. I was so scared that I kept singing, "How Far I'll Go," just to get me through the day so I wouldn't chicken out. Then I was there, and it was like a dream. I learned that Koreans are just like any other people in the world. They get up in the morning, they brush their teeth, they go to work. They love and they fight. They pursue their dreams and have their lazy days. They are just like everyone else, and they do everything that we do with only slight variations. There was nothing to be afraid of. All of my fears now felt irrational. I adjusted quickly to my new environment and forged ahead to have one of the most amazing experiences of my life. I was no longer hindered by past expectations. I was no longer trapped in the box of who I was, or who everyone thought that I should be. I had the freedom to create the person that I wanted to be.

Finally, I was happy, but I wanted more. I wanted to push myself even further. I began my planning and I planned for months right down to the nitty-gritty details of what I wanted to do. I even took a couple mini solo trips to prep myself. I went to the capital of South Korea, Seoul, on my summer break and I went to Okinawa,

Japan between Christmas and New Year's. Then I was ready. I was ready to finally travel solo.

Shuri Castle. Naha, Japan

My Confidence Challenged

Okay...the day is finally here. It is 5 o'clock in the morning on a chilly March day. I am packed and waiting for my taxi. I kiss my boyfriend goodbye, give him a big hug, and tell him that I will message him once I am through security at the airport. I load myself with my lone backpack into the taxi and we are off. We drive at a breakneck speed for the airport. My stomach is quivering with butterflies, so I take deep breaths to stay calm. I communicate a little with my taxi driver, even though my Korean is shaky at best. As the airport comes into view, I remind myself that I can do this. I hop out of my taxi and head into the airport. Pushing confidence into my stride, I march up to the ticket counter. Then my world stops.

"Visa please." says the ticket guy.

"Visa...What visa?" I respond, with my stomach sinking into my feet. The ticket guy looks up at me in a confused way.

"Your visa for Vietnam." He replies slowly.

"I don't have a visa for Vietnam." I reply.

"What do you mean you don't have a visa?" A look of disapproval crossing his features.

"I thought that I could get a visa on arrival for Vietnam." I state hopefully. He lets out a large sigh.

"No, you can't. You must have a visa prior to boarding the plane. Next!"

What have I done? I did everything else, but I didn't think to get a visa. I could have sworn that I could get a visa on arrival in Vietnam just like you can in Cambodia, Thailand, and Laos. It turns out that I was wrong. Shear panic takes over as I begin to realize that my plane is going to leave without me and I have no back-up plan on how to get there. My mind is racing on how I'm supposed to come up with a solution, but my panic is starting to take over. What am I going to do?

Okay, Chelsey. Breathe, just breathe.

I take a deep breath. I slowly go and sit by the wall until I have calmed down. I know that I can figure this out. I have been living by myself for a year in a country where I don't even speak the language. I CAN DO THIS! After I give myself a pep talk, I get the wheels turning in my head.

Okay...What would an adult to do in this situation?

I make my way back to the ticket counter and go up to the guy that I had previously talked to. I asked him what I can do to get to Vietnam. He tells me that I need to go online and get a super priority visa. It will only take a day and I can come back tomorrow. He said that he would be working tomorrow, and he knows that there are plenty of seats open on the airplane for the exact same flight. All I need to do is get the visa, come back the next day, and he would put me on the later plane.

Okay, now I have a plan. I get on the bus to go back home and scramble to get this visa prepared. A realization dawns on me as I'm sitting there. I realize that I just conquered the first major trial of traveling by myself. Something went seriously wrong and I could have just backed out. I could have bagged the entire trip and forgone my dreams because of a simple mistake. Instead, I pulled myself up by my boot straps and kept going. I made it work because I was strong, and I was capable. I could do anything if I put my mind to it. And what do you know? I did it. I got the visa; I adjusted all my travel plans to fit the delay, and I got my butt on that plane the next day. I fixed it and I still got to go on my backpacking dream.

A Whole New World

Over the next 6 weeks I made my way across four different countries through southeast Asia. My trip felt like it was one continuous rollercoaster of events; like there were endless things for me to learn and to see. I started in Hanoi in Northern Vietnam. This wonderful city was vibrant with life. The people had colorful clothes and there were motorcycles zipping by at every turn. I ate my weight in Vietnamese sandwiches and got totally hustled a couple times when trying to buy some new clothes. I quickly learned that to hold my own in Southeast Asia I was going to have to be tough and willing to negotiate, something far from my foreigner brain's normal expectation.

The highlight was taking a tour of Ha Long Bay; but it was not for the stunning rock formations or the fog that made the bay look like something out of a pirate movie. It was the friends that I made. My fear of being completely alone for two months was instantly put to ease when I met some fun loving Dutchies who educated me on the Dutch music scene.

If there is one easy thing that I've noticed about solo travel, it is that you are never truly alone unless you want to be. Backpacking is a social culture and the environment that you're in provides you with hostels, tourist attractions, bars, and other locations that are conducive to making friends. You never have to be worried about meeting people as long as you're willing to reach out, say hi, or just smile at someone new. It was one of these Dutchies who became what I think will be a lifelong friend. I saw him not only on the tour, but an additional two more times throughout my trip.

Ha Long Bay, Vietnam

For the next part of my trip, I went to Ho Chi Minh City and thus began the historical portion of my journey. I began by watching an acrobatics show called Teh Dar at the Opera House. It was an act to demonstrate the culture and beliefs of the Highland People. I was on the edge of my seat for the entire show where I gasped at their daring stunts and almost cried at the emotion they portrayed. I left the Opera House in awe, feeling as though I had stepped back in time and witnessed something beyond my comprehension.

After I had tasted a bit of culture, I moved on to war history. (As a side note: I am a total war history nerd and if there is some kind of war anything when I travel, you can bet that it is highlighted in my itinerary.) I delved in by taking a tour of the Cu Chi Tunnels with a new friend. It was here that the Viet Cong dug tens of thousands of miles of tunnels for their underground networks to house troops, transport war materials, and lay booby traps that could surprise even the most trained soldiers.

At one point I even got to crawl through the tunnels. My friend and I were giggling like mad women as we duck walked through the tight, pitch-black tunnels. It was fun, although exhausting, and painted a happy memory for me. It was not until I visited the War Remnants Museum the next day did I realize the actual atrocities of that war. Walking through the exhibits was as painful as walking on glass. The photographs demonstrated how much tragedy this war had brought and still continues to bring, with the effects of Agent Orange still inflicting generations today. I walked away feeling ashamed of the war my country was in and saddened at all of the unnecessary suffering.

Choeung Ek (The Killing Fields). Phnom Penh, Cambodia

This remorse continued when I crossed into Cambodia to the city of Phnom Penh. Another senseless war was waged here not too long ago, and the country is still pulling itself up from it. I visited the tower of skeletons at the famous Killing Fields as well as the Tuok

Sleng Genocide Center Museum. This is where the prisoners were kept until forced to make a fake confession and then sent to the Killing Fields. It was strange for me because this was something I had never learned about even though it was so recent in history. I had never heard of this war simply because it was so far away and so foreign to what my education deemed necessary. The feeling of enlightenment, of being able to connect with a country through its history was strong, and I was able to more confidently grasp the situation that their country is in and why it looks the way it does. That was not my only revelation in this city.

While lounging in my hostel one afternoon, I met a Finnish man whose accent was equal to Thor. He resonated with me intellectually. We stayed up for hours and talked into the dead of the night. He challenged my way of thinking and made me reevaluate some of the concepts that were so ingrained into who I was. He made me think outside of the box and start questioning myself and my wants. My conversation with him stuck with me for the next week and helped to promote what I think was the start of something new.

Discovering Myself

I had left behind the brutality of war history and was now swinging on a hammock in a bungalow in the southernmost part of Cambodia. The beach was to my left, the jungle to my right, and I had not a care in the world except the book on my lap and my own thoughts.

I sat there for hours thinking about who I was. It was not like The Thinker, with my eyebrows knit and my back hunched in concentration. No. I was swinging sleepily back and forth; the weight of the book on my chest and the sun's warmth in my hair. I was completely isolated in an environment with no external stimuli. I was alone, truly alone for the first time in as long as I could remember. I stayed in my corner of solitude where I was well away from technology. I was away from the pressures of who I thought everyone wanted me to be. I was just me sitting with my thoughts, my dreams, and my aspirations.

Ream National Park in Cambodia

As I sat there, I napped or read my book with the knowledge that nothing needed my attention. I enjoyed the quiet with the birds chirping and the monkeys calling in the distance. All the while, in the back of my mind, the wheels were turning. I looked back upon my life and thought about what truly made me happy. Not what made my boyfriend happy. Not what made my parents happy. Not what made my boss happy or my friends happy. Not even the kind of happy that I thought I should have. Only what made me genuinely happy.

Then the light bulb lit up. An idea began to form and it consumed me. It was all I could think about, and I began planning right then. I began to think about how to make this idea a reality. I had figured out what truly made me the happiest.

I now knew where I wanted to take my life. I never would have had that breakthrough if I had not traveled solo, if I hadn't stepped away from society, if I hadn't taken a breath, if I hadn't let go of everything that was pulling me in so many different directions. None of this would have been possible if I had not taken the moment to look within myself. I had to travel beyond my own borders to be my own self. I had to set aside my fear so that my confidence would have a chance to step up. After making this realization, I stepped out of the box that I had trapped myself in and began to pursue this happiness. That is what solo travel gives you; it gives you the time for reflection and the time to simply be who you are to your core.

Adventure Time

Angkor Wat. Siem Reap, Cambodia

After spending time embracing myself for who I was (cliché, I know), I was so excited to continue on the second half of my trip. I went into Siem Reap and got to explore the creative architecture of the floating villages, the cheap markets where I bought a pair of pants that I never wanted to get out of, and most amazingly was Angkor Wat with that Dutchie from earlier. As I wandered through the ruined temples from centuries ago, with their intricate carvings and craftsmanship that took my breath away, I let my mind wander back in time. I pondered, what were these people thinking? What were they doing? What were their goals and aspirations? Did they just want to get enough food to feed their family? Or were they struggling for a higher purpose, to discover themselves in front of their deity? Were they in love? Were they willing to sacrifice what they wanted for something greater or were they willing to think for themselves and pursue their own dreams? For hours I walked among the ghosts, captured pictures of the present, and thought of what the future held for these long-standing temples.

Then it was back out on my own. I went to Krabi in southern Thailand and to be honest it wasn't that great. The town I went to was a lazy beach town designed for families and tourists who want to soak in the sun. I am not that girl. I'm not a beach bunny who can lay about like a lizard. I am adventurous and a nature lover at heart. It wasn't something that I had realized about myself until then. So, when I quickly grew bored of this city and moved on to the next, that's when my adventuring was put to the test.

I went to northern Thailand, to the city of Chiang Mai, and there I spent three days in full adventure mode. The first day I went ziplining through the jungles. It was crazy to careen hundreds of feet in the air for over three quarters of a mile through the jungle. As I looked down at trees zipping past, I felt like I was flying. It was a rush like none other and as a person who is afraid of heights, afraid of falling, it was a nightmare turned into an amazing dreamland. By the time I was done I was leaping off the platform so that I could go faster on my ride.

The next day I decided to go the other route and instead of careening above the jungle I was now weaving through the water. I went white water rafting, something I've also never done before. I'd never even really been on a river before. My guide and I tipped our way down these rapids while being pushed from side-to-side. I had an excellent guide and he made sure that I was constantly being soaked by water. More than once he took off his own helmet to scoop up water to dump down my back. He was tremendously funny and made me laugh until my belly hurt. I loved the water and the thrill of Mother Nature taking us along was worth it a million times over.

8 Adventures Water Rafting Tour. Chiang Mai, Thailand

My third day of adventuring led me on a quieter path to an elephant sanctuary where I got to learn about elephants that have been used and abused in the most horrific ways. These beautiful and intelligent creatures were scarred forever and struggling to heal but not giving up. Their strength was a testament to their will and how they crave to be alive. It was inspiring to witness their fortitude and an excellent end to my trio of adventuring days.

Movie Moments

While I thought that my adventure days were over, turns out that I was wrong. The following day I decided to head up to Pai, a small mountain village north of Chiang Mai. The adventure didn't begin in the town but in the ride there. It was a 4-hour van ride that felt like a roller coaster. We went zipping around cliffsides up these mountains, playing chicken with giant trucks. Three people in my van, 25% of the passengers, threw up. I managed to hold on to my stomach contents but when we arrived I was about ready to kiss the ground. After all my adventuring, I now had a chance to relax. I had a private bungalow close to the river at a hostel that was very welcoming.

When I arrived though, the owner hustled me down to my room and told me to come right back to the main house. She said we were going to go to the town for a festival and I needed to get dressed. Say what? I had just spent 4 hours praying for dear life after endless adventures; I was exhausted. But...when in Rome, or Pai, I guess. I made my way back up to the main house and she dressed me up like Thai barbie. I had on a long skirt and a long-sleeved shirt despite the wicked heat. My hair was cinched tight in a bun to the back of my head and my neck was weighed down by a gigantic necklace. I wasn't sure what I had gotten myself into. Then I was plunked onto the back of her husband's motorcycle without a helmet and off we went. When we arrived, the streets were filled to the brim. Everyone was dressed in brightly colored clothes, like the ones I had borrowed, and they danced down the street. The festival was in honor of the young boys who were going to study at the temple. These boys were on the shoulders of friends and family as they were paraded down the street amongst all the dancers. They were dressed head to toe in thick makeup and perfect outfits. Even their feet were wrapped in pure white socks that were not allowed to touch the ground until they were set inside the temple itself.

I realized that these were the moments that you hear about in stories. Where travelers are swept up by kind locals and taken on a journey that they will never forget. I will never forget dancing through the street dressed as a local. I will never forget how the locals accepted me with open arms and wanted to take pictures with me or how I got to eat at the temple with all the townsmen as my hostel mum bragged about how I was her daughter. These are the moments that last a lifetime and these movie-like moments did not end here.

After I had my fill of Thailand, I crossed into Laos; all on schedule mind you and it was not what I expected at all. When I had originally planned to go to Laos it was an afterthought, a 6-day tack onto the end of my adventure because I wanted to see as much as I could and as many countries as possible. While I couldn't explore this country as a whole at least I could see one city.

I was in for the most unexpected surprise because what I didn't realize is at this time it was their New Year's. There was a giant water festival for 4 days and I arrived just as it was getting started. For days I was perpetually wet, and the Laotians have no mercy. Unless you go by holding up a camera or a backpack, an obvious display that you don't want it to get wet, they will douse you in water. It is one of their favorite times of the year and they spend it playing in the water like carefree children. It is an utterly freeing experience. There are grandmothers and grandfathers, brothers and sisters, mothers and fathers friends and acquaintances out on the streets playing together with whole-hearted merriment. They line the streets with water guns, hoses, and kiddie pools with the goal of attacking anything that comes within range. I quickly bought some of their waterproof cases to keep my valuables safe as well as a massive super soaking water gun. I was ready to play.

Kuang Si Falls. Luang Prabang, Laos

As a foreigner sometimes you feel uneasy about participating in a celebration of a specific culture if you are not a part of that culture. Just like the people in Pai, these locals accepted me with open arms. They want everyone to experience the joy and renewal of their new year. They laughed, smiled, and had no problem shooting me in the face with a water gun. The kids were the most adamant about it; if they even saw something that moved they would go running after it with a water gun, giggling. Even grandfathers were playing amongst the chaos. One elderly gentleman had joined a group of youthful foreigners with just a small cup. He would come up slowly to you, and gently dump the water on your head. He did it with such ease and kindness that it felt as though he was cleansing away your troubles and purifying you for the new year. He would give you a crooked smile, a slight bow, and then move on to the next youth who needed a calm blessing. You didn't need language to bridge this gap.

 I remember this one moment where I was sitting up on a hill, cherishing the shade on an incredibly hot day. I was lounging there with my giant water gun and taking pictures of the scenes below. Then this little girl came up, her parents are off in the distance, and she's just sat there looking at me. She pointed to my water gun. She didn't say anything; I'm sure even though she was young, she knew my blonde hair and pale skin were not going to be able to answer if she did speak, but she pointed at my water gun with a big smile. I held it up and she nodded. So, I handed it to her and showed her how it worked. She had the biggest grin on her face as she shot some of the water out onto the grass. When she finished, I pointed to her backpack which had a water gun attached to it. She took it out to show me how it worked, and I smiled at her. At that moment, this little girl and I made a connection; even just for five minutes she made a connection with someone not through words or culture or customs but through kindness, generosity, and curiosity. I smiled long after the girl had returned to her parents and thought about how inspiring it was for a little girl to be so open when so much of the world is so closed.

By the time my trip came to an end I was tired. I was ready to go home but I also knew that there was still so much that I had left to see, so much of the world that I wanted to explore, and so many more connections that I wanted to make. It wasn't truly the end of my journey though. While my solo traveling was done for the moment, I had many more trips in the works. I knew that there would be no way that I could remain still for long. Now, though, I knew that I could do anything. I could travel solo. I could go anywhere in the world and no longer needed to wait for others or on my own fears. I was ready. I was ready to be myself. I was ready to follow my dreams. I was ready to pursue my happiness. Are you ready?

Ream National Park, Cambodia

Think Outside the Box

Before I end my tale, I want to tell you of a concept I discovered that had been controlling a part of my life. Not too long ago I talked to one of my dearest friends about a box. This box is the box that society wants to place women in. Now everyone's box is a little bit different, but all these boxes try to contain who we really are.

In some boxes they expect women to have a certain appearance. They want women to mold their bodies to the standards that society has set up for them. They demand that women paint their faces every day, wear perfect clothing, and hobble around on spiky shoes. They tell women to work out not simply because of fitness; but so that we lose weight to become the right shape to wear those tight skirts and the little blouses that men are so fond of. We are told that we must suffer to be beautiful so that we can catch a man. We are then told that it is our fault when a man tries to go too far because we wore the wrong shirt, the wrong skirt, or the wrong makeup.

In other boxes they expect women to be of a certain personality. They want sweetness, patience, and a submissive attitude. They want you to be docile and quiet; catering to the every whim of those you love. They teach women that they need to grow up to be homemakers, to be mothers, to be willing to give up all their hopes and dreams of a career so that they can take care of their family. So that they may cook and clean and host dinner parties. So that they can be a trophy wife while the man gets to go be the breadwinner.

There are many more kinds of these boxes out there. Maybe one where women are supposed to be shy? Supposed to be flirty? Supposed to be bad at math? Supposed to be weak? Slutty? Bubble-brained? Conniving? Blonde? Short? Whatever it may be.

Some of you reading this right now are going, "Say what? That's not true!" You may be lucky, societal boxes may not clutter up your life. Others of you though, are probably nodding, understanding what I mean because you probably live or have lived in some of those boxes. While society is slowly changing to allow women to have more freedom, travel is just barely starting to scrape that surface.

No matter where I went when I traveled through southeast Asia, I kept coming across the same question. They were from girls all over the world; Sweden, Mexico, United States, Korea, Canada and more. All of these girls were asking, "Where's your friend? Where's your boyfriend? Where's your husband?" and "Why is nobody here with you?" At first, I was offended. Why should I need someone with me? I've traveled with people before and I want to do this by myself. Then they would ask, "Are you not worried?" or "Aren't you scared? It's not safe here by yourself."

Again, I was offended, but then I got worried. I began to worry about whether I should be here by myself. Should I not be alone? Should I be scared? Then I realized that all of these women were stuck inside of that box and that they wanted to put me there too because it's normal and predictable. That box is nowhere where I want to be.

I told them with confidence that I can travel by myself. That I am strong. That I am safe as long as I am smart. Of course, some people can be bad but bad people live everywhere in the world. Most people will be there to help you if you're willing to ask for it. While the world can be scary, as long as you're smart then you are strong enough to do anything that you want to do. I made it a goal to help women get out of this box, to help them learn that they are smart, to help them understand that they are capable, and let them know that even if everything goes to hell they can find their way back. Women are resilient, they are strong, they are capable, and they don't need someone to hold their hand for their entire life and to give them permission on what they can or can't do.

So, I ask you...Are you ready? Are you ready to see the world through your own eyes? Are you ready to be whoever you want to be? Are you ready to do whatever feels right to you? Are you ready to discover who you are without that box? Are you ready to have an experience that you will never forget? If the answer is no, that is ok. You will get there when you are ready. If the answer is yes, then it is time. It is time for you to travel solo. It is time for you to be bold, be brave, and be wise.

"Well behaved women rarely make history."
~ **Eleanor Roosevelt**

Chelsey Schultz

Chelsey is currently living a nomadic lifestyle. She travels the world by pet sitting and working as a freelance ESL teacher. She has been to 21 countries in the past two years and does not plan on slowing down anytime soon. She is passionate about reading, being outdoors, and eating as much chocolate as possible. Most of all, Chelsey loves martial arts. She is a second-degree black belt in Uechi-Ryu Karate and is a self-defense instructor. In her free time, she runs a travel safety blog as well as a Facebook group on travel safety for women.

Blog: https://theninjagypsy.com
Facebook Group:
http://www.facebook.com/safetravelforwomen
Instagram: https://www.instagram.com/theninjagypsy